Poems –
Songs and Letters

Poems -
Songs and Letters

Volume I

Keith Vance

POEMS - SONGS AND LETTERS: VOLUME I

This book is written to provide information and motivation to readers. Its purpose is not to render any type of psychological, legal, or professional advice of any kind. The content is the sole opinion and expression of the author, and not necessarily that of the publisher.

Copyright © 2019 by Keith Vance

All rights reserved. No part of this book may be reproduced, transmitted, or distributed in any form by any means, including, but not limited to, recording, photocopying, or taking screenshots of parts of the book, without prior written permission from the author or the publisher. Brief quotations for noncommercial purposes, such as book reviews, permitted by Fair Use of the U.S. Copyright Law, are allowed without written permissions, as long as such quotations do not cause damage to the book's commercial value. For permissions, write to the publisher, whose address is stated below.

Printed in the United States of America.

ISBN   978-1-64552-138-9   (Paperback)
ISBN   978-1-64552-139-6   (Digital)

Lettra Press books may be ordered through booksellers or by contacting:

Lettra Press LLC
18601 Green Valley Ranch Blvd.
Unit 108, Box 204 Denver, CO 80249
1 303 586 1431 | info@lettrapress.com
www.lettrapress.com

Contents

Dedication ix
Major Players xi
Preface xv
Introduction xvii

A "God" Conversation 1
I Think About Jesus 2
"This Cross" 3
"From A Sinner To A Winner" 4
I Will Hear My Mother Praise The Lord Again 6
devil Don't Waste Your Time On Me 8
"Wrap Me Jesus" 9
"By Fire The Next Time" 11
"Reflections" 12
"Here's To It" 13
A Glimpse At An Old Soldiers Heart 14
"The Confederate Battle Creed" 16
"For Love And Liberty" 18
"One Who Dares" 19
"Run Boy Run" 20
"Life Parts" 21
Play Around In Your Own Backyard 22
"When You Know What You Know" 23
You Watch My Dreams Come True 24
"My Imagination" 25
"I'm Going To Do Now" 26
"Citizens of----------------" [1st letter] 28
"The "Ole" Red Creek Store" 31
"A Rose For Mother" 34
"A Spark Of Love" 35
"Phantom Lover" 36
"Loving You Is What I Do" 37

Eighteen Years And Eighteen Roses	38
"Pure"	39
"Not That I Care For Her"	40
"Lady Love"	42
"Citizens of------------"	43
"Love Questions" #1	44
"Pay No Mind"	45
"Why Can't It Be Me"	46
"Small Wonder"	47
"A Poet-Or-Writers Nightmare"	48
Dirty Black Coal	49
"Staten Island Blues"	50
"Barefoot And Pregnant"	52
"Keep The Lid On The Bottle"	53
"A Dollar A Shot"	54
"Pen And Phone"	55
"The Days Of Poe"	56
"Oh Virginia"	57
"My Friend, Mr. Cho"	59
"For Tam"	60
"To Danielle"	61
"To Kristeen"	62
"Father Time"	63
"Father Time"	64
"Stacey My Bartending Lady"	66
I'm Tired Of Being Everybody's Man	68
"To Keith"	69
"To Donna"	70
"For Karen"	71
"Loves End"	72
"Cheat River Bride"	73
"Playing Love Games"	75
Dry Cleaning Route-Man Super-Star	77
"To Mary Jane"	78
"The One That Got Away"	79
"Visions Of A Girl"	80

"Such A Little Kingdom"...81
"I Am Looking" #2..81
"Hey Ruka"..82
"Lost Treasure"..84
"Side-Saddle"...85
"I Just Can't Go"...86
"Lost"..88
"I'd Venture To Say"...89
"It's Not Over For Me"..90
"My Chosen Memories"..91
"Don't Feel Sorry For Me"..93
"Someone You Never Knew"...94
"I'll Be Waiting Here At Home"..96
"When You've Gone"..97
"What You Make Of Me"...98
"All These Things"...99
"She Sings Love Songs"...100
"Mixed Emotions"...101
"Sadness"...102
"Mental Misery"..103
"No More"...104
"You Had, Your Chance But You Blew It"...............................105
"I Just Couldn't Care Less"...106
"A Lesson In Love"...107
"The Easy Way Out"..108
"Don't Fool With Danger"..109
"Benbush"..110
"I Picked Up the Wrong End Again"...111
"Raining From My Georgia Skies"...112
"Sweet Young Country Girl"..113
"One Weakness"...114
"Someone I Knew"...115
"Don't Take Her"..116
"Mr. Heartache"..117
"Lay Your Lovn' Down"...118
When Someone Beaks The Bad News To Me..........................119

"Without Saying Goodbye" 120
"Don't Wake Me" 121
"Love And Farewell" 122
"A Picture Of Me" 124
"She's Still Rockin' This Ship" 125
"A Letter Of Teardrops" 126
"Brown Eyes Long Hair" 128
"Think About Me" 129
The Tears On My Pillow Never Dry 130
"I Love To Dream" 131
"Down Memory Row" 132
"Brand-new Birthday Blues" 134
"Love Questions #2" 136
"Thanks-Love" 137
Looks A Whole Lot Better Leavin' 138
"Put A Bell On My Bottle" 139
"The All American Drunk" 140
"Illegal Brew" 141
Think Maybe I'll Find Myself Here 142
"The Fear Of Dying" 144
"Gonna Drink Up All The Beer" 144
West Virginia Made An Alkie Out-A-Me 146
Alcohol – From My Head To My Toe 147
The Bottles Are Empty – The Tables Are Bare 149
"No Room In My Belly For A Beer" 150
Rooster 151
"The Wanton Of Death" 152

Dedication

Volume #1 of POEMS-SONGS and LETTERS, is dedicated to all the people who played a part in providing me with a topic to write about, or gave me a reason to write. Their names are very important to me, but need not be disclosed. They will know who they are, if or when they read it.

This book's proceeds will be donated to a small Church of "God" in Hamilton Virginia, and the Wounded Warrior program. That little church, found quite by accident, it's congregation and pastor Paul Campbell and his wife Geneva played a very special and important part in my life. At a time when changes were taking place at an uncontrollable pace I learned to let go and let "God" do his job.

"God" gave me the talent to put words together and provided me with the opportunity to live in a free world that would allow publication regardless of content. So I give thanks to "God" for once again showing his mercy, grace, and favor in guiding me through life by properly placing this little church, its pastor and congregation for me in my time of need. The tithing amount of 10% of the proceeds of this book will be given to the Abundant Life Ministries Church of "God", located at 39041 East Colonial Hwy., or Box 420, Hamilton, VA 20159, Just in case anyone purchasing this book would like to experience the blessing of a lifetime, I guarantee you will feel at home and be welcome there. Or if you would like to support their cause in that community it will do your heart good, and your harvest will be blessed. An additional 10% will be given to this same church, to be used for what ever they feel necessary to help them achieve their goals. Thank you for being there for me. I love you all, and "God" bless you.

The Wounded Warriors, **I can not say enough!!!** If not for them, fighting, losing life and limb for the freedom and rights of this great country, and around the world. My life as I have known it would not have been possible. Without hesitation, they proudly wore the uniforms and flags of this country. They risked everything so we might have everything, and enjoy the pleasures of a life they quite possibly will never have. And that would be a full and complete life in a free country.

The Wounded Warriors program will receive 80% of the proceeds from this book. My "God", I hope and pray, this book makes a billion dollars. If that were to be so, I would still be indebted to them. Thanks to "God", and this great nation that was birthed under "God", along with these totally unselfish and undeniably brave soldiers, I have been afforded a life that identifies with a good dream.

And so to "God", to the many soldiers who gave their lives, and to every present soldier, every veteran, and to all the Wounded Warriors of these United States and its allies, that fought in my place to preserve its liberty and freedom. I say THANK YOU! THANK YOU!

THANK YOU!!! And may "God" bless you all as He has done for me.

Sincerely

Keith Vance

Major Players

I would like to spend a moment and take a few lines to thank all of my immediate family, a very special cousin, some friends that fell into the right places along the way, and one of the best friends, if not the best friend I have ever had, for the part they played in my life.

First and foremost, I would like to say thank you to a young lady that is very special, and played a most important part in assisting me with my inadequate, to say the least, computer skills. She displayed the patience of "saint", and I believe she is one. Thank you so very much!!! Ms. Ella Jayme

Though my mother and father have passed away, they both influenced me in a very positive way. They always protected me, encouraged, and gave guidance when they felt it necessary. Their memory lives with me.

As for my brothers and sisters, I shall try to put them in order by age beginning with the oldest: Roberta, Dennis, myself, Bobby, Teddy, Charlotte, Larry, Shelby, and Barbara. I have always looked to and appreciated you with highest regards and deepest heart felt emotions. Although we were seldom geographically close, which was mostly my fault because of my wandering ways, I always felt a closeness of heart; and when we did get together occasionally, it was more than obvious that you all felt the same way. I thank every one of you for the love and kindness you have shown me throughout my life. I would also like to thank you for your understanding and forgiving ways when I would go a little crazy from time to time. Know that you are in my heart, my thoughts, my prayers, my dreams, and on every page of this book. Without all of you, this dream would have not been realized.

[AND THEN THERE WAS WILLIE]

Willie Nelson:

one morning about 3 or 4 a.m., in the late 50s, maybe 58 or 59, I was lying on my bed writing and listening to W-C-K-Y Cincinnati-1 Ohio, 1530 on you're a.m. radio dial. I believe the DJ's name was Wayne Rainey. He suddenly broke into commentary about this up and coming young songwriter that was going to make it big someday. And how he was so far ahead of his time, then he played it, and I knew he was right. "I had not planned on seeing you, I was afraid of what I'd do, but pride is strong here am I, and I just can't let you say goodbye." Lines like; "what force behind your evil mind, can let your lips speak so unkind." Then there was; "the flesh around your throat is pale, intended by my fingernails." **"I Just Can't Let You Say Goodbye"** I set up in bed and said, "damn, this guy is a poet first and a songwriter second, he writes the way I do". I never forgot Willie, or that song they both helped me a lot. Wayne Rainey proved to be right, Willie made it bigger than big. Which also told me that I had been right for writing down my every thought. Thank you Willie for being there in those early morning hours to help me along.

And now I have a very special debt of thanks to my first cousin, Eugene Roy. Eugene provided me, at a very young age, the opportunity to drive off into the sunset and continue to follow my dreams. And that is exactly what I did without looking back, and what a dream world I drove into. Eugene, you were always in my thoughts and prayers, as you are today. I love ya man!!! Thank you for helping me, and for the part you have played in the creation of my memoirs. You were always the best mechanic, and cousin I knew.

Ray Shrout:

He was a childhood friend whose mother made the best peanut butter and jelly sandwiches in town.

Pauletta King:
My beautiful neighbor, she married Ray and we became lifelong friends. Now I eat Pauletta's peanut butter and jelly sandwiches. If it were not for Pauletta's literary expertise this book would have 10 times as many mistakes as it may have now. We had our own painting and moving company, and I cannot tell you how many times I have ended up sleeping on their couch. Words cannot express my appreciation of your friendship. Ray and Pauletta, thanks for being there, I love you both.

Sen. Jay O'Brien:
He worked with me and became a good friend while guiding me through the political and legislative process of getting bills passed. He worked hard enough to succeed in getting 18 out of 31 passed unanimously in a 15 year time frame. He was batting over 500 and that's a good average.
Jay you are a good man, I really miss working with you.
Thank you my friend for being there.

Mark Werblood:
He was, and still is my attorney, and came on the scene in the early 90s. He became a friend I could trust, go to lunch with, laugh and joke about some of the ridiculously stupid ideas I would have. He had a sense of humor that lightened the seriousness of the moment.
Thanks for being there Mark.
P.S. don't forget what is to happen at my final party.

I would like to thank Dave Hudnall for his computer expertise and for his patience and eagerness to make all the changes necessary, created by the mistakes I made. He worked diligently to eliminate the do-overs I insisted on as we were putting this book together.

And last, but certainly not least, my thanks and appreciation go out to a very good and dear friend of mine from high school days, Ms. Wilma Lantz. Wilma provided me the luxury of all the privacy and solitude necessary to accomplish my goal. It was utterly impossible to disturb me. It was like I was under lock and key with a shotgun guard. I never thought incarceration could be so much fun. I went from 180 pounds to 206, from black to snow white hair, and from a nondrinker to an alcoholic and back again twice. From suits and ties to bib overalls and ponchos, I became a number one advocate of white – lightning and moon – shine. This would become obvious in the lyrics of some of my songs. So if you are of mind to come looking for me, don't! You would have better luck getting into Fort Knox, than through my front door. I sometimes can't even find myself, this will also surface in lyrics. Seriously Wilma, or, Willa Mae, none of this would have been possible if not for you. I will be forever in your debt my dear. Thank you so very much, love ya girl!!!

Preface

This book of poems songs and letters formulation process began when I was quite young. I remember making up or creating situations to write about. Some good, some bad, some dangerous, and some were impossible. By the time I was a sophomore in high school I had amassed quite a collection, which was stored, either in memory or my composition books. I was very fortunate to have the best sophomore English teacher in the world. Her name was Mrs. Mary Kee. When she read some of my pieces, knowing the value of encouragement, she told me I was a born writer. I have never forgotten Mrs. Kee, or what she said. I think of her daily with the question. "I wonder if Mrs. Kee would like, or approve of this one?" From that day forward putting words together was an easy thing for me to do. A pencil and paper, and later many different kinds of tape recorders became a part of my everyday attire. I had them in my pockets, placed under my car seat, spare ones in the glove box, taped under the dining room table, under my pillow and under my bed. By the time I retired in 2013, I had 7 books in the making – over 200 letters, and thousands of poems and songs, all of which, by the grace of "God" Almighty, I intend to publish within the next five years. Apart from that I co-authored 31 bills that were presented to the Virginia legislature, out of which 18 passed with very little opposition. These bills were directed to the betterment of driver education and driver improvement in the state of Virginia. Many of these requirements and regulations were adopted by other states across the country, and Virginia became known as the pioneer state in the field of driver education.

I've always loved to write. Poetry came natural to me. I love poetry, especially of the Elizabethan period, even if I don't write many sonnets. There was only one man of sonnets. Still I believe poetry of all kind should be brought more to the forefront. It seems today that everyone is a writer and poetry is a lost art. However, there are ways of reviving that lost art. For example, if the host of every talk show, or even a newscaster every now and then, were to somehow incorporate just one poem, good, bad, or indifferent (after all, who is to say what is good or bad or indifferent) that would certainly help in bringing poetry back to life. But I suppose that's just a poet lover's pipedream. I for one believe everyone should have more dreams. I rather doubt there is anyone who has realized their every dream, but perhaps the more dreams we have, the more we can make come true. That particular dream could serve as a monotony breaker from the same – old / same – old – B/S we usually hear on talk shows. So how about it talk show hosts, you guys are intelligent, I know you could come up with something that works for your show. When you get right down to it, poetry is a feel-good kind of literature. Even the tear-jerking, morbid ones, made most of their authors feel better from the value of releasing inner feelings. So give your viewers a little feel-good time, besides it's fun to make things rhyme, right Gutfeld.

Introduction

We begin with religious pages then lead into normal everyday poetry, patriotic, letters, work, love and tears. We end with drinking and dying.

The intent is to present a mix of easy to read, and also easy not to read poems and songs that you may or may not want to read.

Please keep in mind, a writer cannot squash that which flows from mind to paper.

A "God" Conversation

(at 4:00 a.m.)
4-19-14

I thank you Lord "God", for making me everything that I am
and giving me everything I have, or, have ever had.
These things come from you as a gift to me, and I thank you "God".
You have made me in the image of you. The problem begins when
you exhibit some of your masterful "Godly" ways, I feel that I
must do the same!
Failing feverishly of course, barely reaching number one on a
scale of one through ten.
Help-me-out-here, do you think possibly
a characteristic resembling rebelism, could have come
from your emotional expoundations of love to my ears?

Tell me Lord "God", what do you want from me?
I am yours and always have been.
Without you my life would have been nothing.
With you, my life has been everything I have ever needed and more.
I hold nothing or no/one above you, though my
daily life is as un/forgiven as life itself.
That is the part of me, that is not, my "God", to say that I am right,

but more of the desire to be understood for my
ability to interpret your messages to me.

May you grant me the grace, the mercy, the faith,
the belief, and the true meaning of loving my fellow man
so that I might glorify you in ways that only
you could make come true.
"God", Almighty one, I come to you with sin-filled mannerisms.

Take from me the unholy thoughts, and
my covetous ways. Make me pure and make me true, for I
have only one "God", and that, Jehovah Jireh, is you!!!
(my prayer is)
Heavenly Father, I ask your forgiveness, your direction,
and protection, in and throughout my life. I ask you to bless my work,
in ways that it may serve as a blessing and comfort to others.
I ask these things, "Father God", in your son's holy name
in Jesus precious name, I pray, Amen!!!

I Think About Jesus

2009

Oh the nice thing about Jesus
He is always around
And the nice thing about Jesus
He will never let you down
Yes the nice thing about Jesus
He is a true friend to be found
Oh the really nice thing about Jesus
He will make sure, you're heaven bound

could be used as a beginning praise song

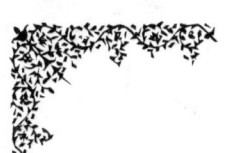

"This Cross"

4-25-13

This cross I wear as a memory
Of "The Cross" Jesus bore when He set me free;
This cross reminds me of the suffering and pain,
From the weight on <u>"His Shoulders"</u>, while clearing my name;
This cross holds the story of a hammer and nails, And
The sounds of screaming as so many tears fell;
This cross tells me, that <u>"He Is My King"</u>,
With a crown of thorns, <u>"His Blood Cleansed Everything"</u>;
This cross is my guide, and it keeps me on track,
In search of tomorrow, and not looking back;
This cross gives me the peace, of <u>"His Redeeming Grace"</u>,
It's a constant reminder, of the <u>"Love In His face"</u>;
While being nailed to a cross with a crown of thorns,
Smitten by swords, laughed at and scorned;
I will never stop holding, to the hand that holds mine,
For this cross holds the story, that will out–last time;
This "cross" gives me peace, this "cross" helps me find,
The love of my "Savoir" is heaven divine;
This "cross" shows me grace, and I don't worry anymore,
<u>For I know I'll see Jesus, on "God's" Golden shore.</u>

"From A Sinner To A Winner"

2008
Song

Oh "God", help me, I am a sinner; keep me in thy grace.
Teach me to walk in the light
Every day and night,
Until I can look upon your face.

And on that day, I'll be a winner;
I'm going to ride that gospel ship across the sky.
For it is written in a story;
That is where we will spend sweet by and by.

I have a lot of problems here in this life,
Though most of them I brought up on myself.
But Jesus washed my sins a way
And on that very day
He put all my burdens on a shelf.

Yes "God" blessed me when I was a sinner.
He kept me in his grace.
He taught me to walk in the light
Every day and night
And now I can look upon His face.

And I know now I am a winner;
I'm going to ride that gospel ship across the sky.
For it is written in a story;
That is where we will spend sweet by and by.

So if things are going bad for you in your life,
And you just can't seem to understand,
Take it to the Lord in prayer
And He will help you there.
He will put it in the Masters hands.

Yes, he will put it in the hands
Of the one that made the plan,
Jesus – – will – – put it – – in
The – –Masters – – hands.

Oh, and on that day you'll be a winner;
You can ride that gospel ship across the sky.
For it is written in the Bible;
That is where we will spend sweet by and by.

Yes "God" blessed us all cause we were sinners.
He keeps us in His grace.
He taught us to walk in His light every day and night,
And now we can look upon His Face.
Oh, – – someday – – soon – – we – – shall – –
See – – our – –Savior's –face!!!

I Will Hear My Mother Praise The Lord Again

9-18-2009
Song

Oh she prayed for me when my life was filled with sin;
She prayed for my forgiveness, and to let my Savior in.
She didn't live long enough to see what Jesus did for me;
Oh, He opened up my heart and walked right in
----------[talk]----------
{and then He told me}
---------[sing]----------
You will hear your mother praise the Lord again;
Yes, you will hear her tender voice and then-

Oh, how happy you will be, that you finally came to me;
you will hear your mother praise the Lord again.

Now I wouldn't listen to things she'd say,
Because I thought that I was whole within;
But when I realized it wasn't so,
I tried to let my Jesus know;
Then He said, that account was settled long ago.
And you will hear your mother praise the Lord again;
Yes, you will hear her tender voice and then-
Oh, how happy you will be, that from sin I set you free;
You will hear your mother praise the Lord again.

Yes, I will hear my mother praise the Lord again,
Since Jesus came into my life, and took away all my sins.
Now I'm on my way to heaven, when I leave this world behind,
I want to hear my mother's praises one more time.
-time after time-

My mother worked her fingers to the bone,

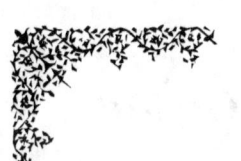

Because she had to raise us on her own.
She had great big calluses on her knees;
They came from praying, pulling weeds, and planting trees.

With her every waking moment came a prayer,
And I know someday I'll meet her over there.
Oh, how happy she will be, to see her praying got to me;
And I will hear my mother praise the Lord again.
She will thank Him for forgiving all my sins.
We'll walk through heaven hand in hand,
Thanking "God" for His great plan;
And I will hear my mother praise the Lord again.

My mother went to church and "praised the Lord,"
Her tithes was anything she could afford.
I held her hand and tried not to cry,
As she went to her new home on high;
Where we will all be together by-and-by,
And I will hear my mother praise the Lord again.

Yes, I will hear my mother praise the Lord again,
Since Jesus came into my life and took away all my sins.
Now I'm on my way to heaven when I leave this world behind;
I want to hear my mother's praises one more time.
-time after time-
Oh yes, I will hear my mother praise the Lord again;
I will hear her tender voice and then-
Oh, how happy she will be, that from sin I've been set free;
And I will hear my mother praise the Lord again.
[softer and lower]
Yes, I will hear my mother praise the Lord again.

devil Don't Waste Your Time On Me

4-8-71
Song

devil, don't you waste your time on me;
Can't you see the gold and silver on my wings?
Well I'm on my way to glory,
And that you can't destroy;

So – devil, don't you waste your time on me.

I don't want you hanging around no more;
That shoulder you been leaning on is getting mighty sore.
I'm as clean as I can be,
Thank "God" my soul is free;

So – devil don't you waste your time on me.

Now you've been knocking at my door trying to get in,
Cause you thought I was tied in slavery to your world of sin.
But you will be surprised;
Jesus filled my soul with pride.
And with Him holding me you just can't win,
So – devil don't you waste your time on me.

Get behind me, like you're supposed to be,
For I'm walking with my Savior can't you see;
Yes, He built a home in heaven,
And He built it just for me;

So – devil don't you waste your time on me. Can't you see the gold and silver on my Wings?
Well I'm on my way to glory, And that can't destroy;
So – devil don't you waste your time on me.

"Wrap Me Jesus"

[with your wonderful love]
October – 2009
Chorus

Oh, wrap me Jesus with your wonderful love
Yes wrap me Jesus with your wonderful love
Send down your Spirit from above,
and wrap me Jesus with your wonderful love
Oh, wrap me Jesus with your wonderful love
yes wrap me Jesus with your wonderful love
Tell Saint Peter what I'm dreaming of,
and wrap me Jesus with your wonderful love

I'm dreaming of heaven, I'm dreaming of lovin',
i'm dreaming of a whole lot of up – abovin'
When the Spirit moves, I don't need a shove
so wrap me Jesus with your wonderful love

Chorus
I'm dreaming of a mansion and streets of gold.
I'm dreaming of a land, where we never grow old.
I've got a one-way ticket, up above.
So wrap me Jesus with your wonderful love.

Chorus
I'm dreaming of a place with no sorrow and strife
i want to see my name, in the Lamb's book of life
Doing everything right, is what I'm dreaming of
so wrap me Jesus with your wonderful love

Chorus
I'm dreaming of touching my Jesus' hand
then I'll know I'm part of, the Master's plan
We will walk those streets, hand in hand
when "God" takes us home, to our promised land

Chorus

background lyrics to all chorus's
wrap me, wrap me, wrap me Jesus; wrap me, wrap me, wrap me Jesus;
wrap me, wrap me, wrap me Jesus; Jesus wrap me with your love.

<u>{repeat in background throughout the chorus with lower voice:}</u>
<u>{coordinate to finish at the same time as the chorus finishes:}</u>

"By Fire The Next Time"

2-23-14
{at 2 AM}

I guess some people don't understand,
The words He spoke in His commands-
Evil, filth, and corruption, was not part of the plan;
He let some things slip by, then it got out of hand.
So "God" told Noah, make yourself a boat,
And you build it large enough to float.
You gather me animals of every breed,
So on this new earth there will be new seed.
Everything bad was destroyed back then,
So mankind and earth could begin again.
This transformation was a punishing time,
Because "God" don't like it when you step out of line.
He said, "I Am Alpha and Omega I caused this to begin,
And <u>I Am</u> the One who will bring it to an end".
For many long days and nights Noah hung on,
Sometimes it seemed like all hope was gone;
But just about the time he started to give up,
A bird came back and dropped a leaf in his cup.
This was the proof somewhere there was land,
And it was all part of "God's" great plan.
And so the ark came to rest and life there was new,
Then "God" told Noah what his people had to do.
"Obey my commandments I have written them in stone.
If they should fail to heed, their fate they will own.
I have much love for my creation,
On which I will build families and nations;
But if my laws are disobeyed and obedience declines,
I shall destroy it again, **but by fire the next time**"!!!
{Praise "GOD" amen and amen}

The prophecy is of the days we are living in,
When the people in charge are power – hungry women and men.
Some have half – a – mind, and others have none;
Someday they will answer for the wrongs they've done-
For the people they killed and the lies they told,
Just because they can, from the office they hold.
For the bombs they drop and chalk it up to war;
War leaves nothing, the way it was before.
It makes them feel they have a powerful hand,
So they try in every way, to destroy "GODS" plan.
But their hands are weak and so is their mind,
And someday soon, they're all going to find;
There's only one hand with that control,
It's the hand of the <u>Man</u>, <u>that owns our soul</u>!!!

"Reflections"

5-27-87

it's an early morning sunrise on a far and distant shore
it's a midnight masquerade that doesn't matter anymore
it's about a man and woman who could not make the score
it's a country standing tall though it's battle scarred and torn
it's the chill and bump experience when the national anthem plays
it's the history of this country that leaves us all amazed
it's an international message that we all should understand
it's the silence screams throughout the night for unity of man
it's the wind that blows "old glory" and snaps her like a whip
it's the hand that rules the world to make sure we don't slip
it's the facing of our daily chores whether we fly or till the sod
for all these things we can be thankful,
to an Almighty ever loving, "God"!!!

"Here's To It"
1958

here's to the little Robin red breast
a cheerful sign of spring

here's to the lucky bride – to – be
who has just received a ring

here's to the nation's Air Force
and all the planes they fly

here's to all the heavenly bodies
that brighten up the sky

here's to a great nation
that shall never fall
here is to America
with freedom unto all

A Glimpse At An Old Soldiers Heart

8-10-1963

you see son the battle is over, we fought hard but still we have lost

this dispute that split our nation, took the life
of many – a – good man at its cost

as – a – matter – of – fact, we paid a great price
for this battle, the South and the North

yeah, son it's the truth, we paid more, so much more than it was worth

but you see boy, that's the thing about fightin' a war

you don't take time to stop and think, is this really worth it to me

you just go right on ahead fightin' son, it's not about you

you're fighting for the things you've come to believe

and that boy, is one of the best things we have in this nation

we can believe in what we think is right

and in this case son, there was no better way to show our belief
than just to get right out there and fight

for if you don't stand up, and keep right on
standin' up for what you believe

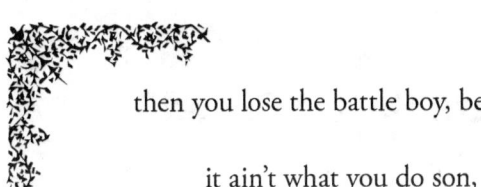
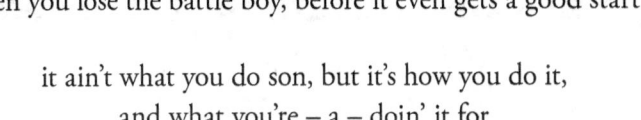

then you lose the battle boy, before it even gets a good start

it ain't what you do son, but it's how you do it,
and what you're – a – doin' it for
now that's what gives ya the satisfaction of heart

so listen son, before you pass judgment on them Yankees

you just give a little mind to the things your pa had to say

yeah it's true boy, they won the battle at a very high price

it took-em nigh on to four years, to conquer the blue and gray

aw-, but we got a good country now son

one that's right able to hold its own

and we ought to be proud boy, yeah real proud

to be part of this freedom lovers land we call home

you know son, maybe someday before too long

all the people in this country, maybe they'll believe in the same thing

and I hope that day comes real soon boy

cause I'm – a thinkin' of all the happiness it'll bring

"The Confederate Battle Creed"

5-16-61

till this battle we are fighting
has been marked for history

I shall ever press forward
for those cheers of victory

I will not stand by
and let a northern man

march across the soil
of this sacred southern land

I will always stand up bravely
for our fighting cause I see

never once shall I turn and run
from a no – good damn Yankee

until this "ole" southern body
has brought forth its last breath

shall I permit a northern soldier
to trod this southern earth

I will fight with the utmost courage
and all of my ability

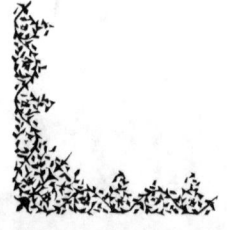

I will always stand behind
and backup general Lee

by the grace of "God" Almighty
whom I shall meet at the pearly gates

I will be forever faithful
to these Confederate states

for the very reason
these states were torn apart

gives me every right to be
a rebel at heart

and if necessary, a rebel I will die
with my rifle in my hand

but live or die I shall be proud
to have served the South-land

"For Love And Liberty"
1967-68

the battle was raging, the shells flying by
men crying, dying, and we all wonder why

oh "God" up in heaven, the answer if you will
were we born to love, or were we born to kill

I cannot help but wonder, as we do, of the heavens above
no silence to see, only pain and agony, where is the love

why did we come here, to a land not our own
when we could all be living a peaceful life at home

the battlefields are bloody, the heroes are all dead
no chaplain to hear, the last words they said

yes, "God" has the answer, the love of freedom and liberty
for years, men have been dying, men like you and me

so I cannot say I don't know, the reason why I am
helping fight this battle, over here in Vietnam

"One Who Dares"

12-15-63

one who dares to acquire both fortune and fame
one who lives to achieve, to accomplish, to gain

one who sets his goals, and then takes aim
one whose self – confidence exploits his name

one who accepts love and kindness
but returns none of the same

one whose knowledge of love is limited
to his own personal domain

one who takes love but never yields
to his lover in the game

one who cuts a heart so deeply
yet never takes the blame

one whose thoughts are only of himself
and puts all others to shame

one who glory hunts
and the wildest creatures he does tame

one whose pride to himself is great
but in others eyes 'tis lame
        {this <u>one</u> will conquer fortune, fame, and himself}

"Run Boy Run"

1-4-71
Song

when trouble starts to follow you
well here's the one thing you can do
pack up your bags and follow through
run boy run
run boy run, run for the sun
your settling days are done
so start running boy and run

get on that bus with a ticket in your hand
you're heading out for your wonderland

tell nobody where you're going
tell nobody where you're from
the less you say and you'll keep it that way
so--run boy run

don't look over your shoulder
until you get a little older
or it will cause confusion in your plan
keep your eye on your goals
and be true to your soul
and don't get in trouble with the man

keep moving like a magic man make
sure you always have a plan
and that includes having a lot of fun

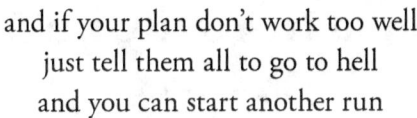

and if your plan don't work too well
just tell them all to go to hell
and you can start another run

yeah – – run boy run run
boy run, run for the sun
your settling days are done
so start running boy and run
run boy run

"Life Parts"

5-25-80

tonight I am so sad as I think of mom and
dad all alone with no one to care
the county is taking their home for taxes
life to them has been unfair
these prison walls are hell when you're trying to
tell your mother and father you care
there is no way I can say just how I feel today
while breathing incarcerated air
loving and working is all they ever knew
church-going people, to "God" they were true
and now that they are older and living is hard
"God", why must I be held under guard

IF YOU HAD CARED SO BEFORE
GOOD MEMORIES WOULD BE YOURS

Play Around In Your Own Backyard
12 – 15 – 63

we search for the evil in others
the more we look the more we find
we think, my how dreadful, a man of this nature
I sure hope there are few of his kind
should we look for the goodness or only the bad
should we think a man filled with evil
what good points could he have
just remember while you're searching
you may have faults of your own
so why not search your own heart
and let this poor wretch alone
if you think evil qualities in you do not exist
no use looking, for there is none to find
you are so wrong for thinking this
or could it be to your faults you are blind
closed eyes closes minds to one's own ways
we see just what we want it to be
how long can we keep pulling the shades
thinking no one else can see
it might be difficult in the beginning
but if we look surely we can find
to stay only in tune with winning
is proof of how narrow the mind
now we know everyone is not of evil senses
but being capable of evil deeds is not hard
so before crossing your neighbors fences
try playing around in your own backyard

"When You Know What You Know"

4-3-71

when you know what you know then you know it
all you have to do is go right out and show it
but if you don't do it right you will blow it
but you can do it every time if you know it

a man among men once thought he was the greatest
well I don't know if you've heard the
latest

he found out about being great a little late
but when the time is right he'll set it straight

seems he bit off too much and he just couldn't chew it
he knows a lot more now than when he thought he knew it

although it was a blow
his appearance clearly shows
he knows so much more
then he knew before
no he did not suffer defeat
instead a mental victory he did meet
from this lesson he will learn
each man is paid for what he earns

his reward was a little poor
and his ego kind of sore
he will be back for more
now he's better than before

and he has only left, to show it
for he knows what he knows and he knows it

You Watch My Dreams Come True

1963

you watch my dreams come
true and yes, I'll show them all to you
everything you said I couldn't do I'll do
it over to prove that it's true time will revive your memory
everything I said is what I'll be
you told me I was a dreamer
so I shall be your dream-weaver
I've got news for you my dear
my promise will be very clear
this dreamer just made up his mind
my dreams are never hard to find
you're always finding faults in me
not even once did you believe
what I wanted could ever be
anything short of a fantasy
you'll be surprised at what I can do
you just watch my dreams come true

"My Imagination"
1957

while I sit beside this brook
reading from a little book

my imagination disappears
and wanders to the by-gone years

what I see in this spellbound state
could be no less than an act of fate

at the throne of a king I cast my sword
then came the cry, "oh Lord! Dear Lord!"

What have I done, I know not why
I've killed the King, I'll surely die

to the courtyard, they took me quick
and placed my neck across a stick

with my head held firmly on one side
I cried, "alas! Why must I die

the axman held his ax up high
but then before my fatal cry

my imagination it did die
and left me with an empty eye

this King I killed, where was he from
I found out not from whence he'd come

my mind was filled with fascination
thus I know, 'twas my imagination

"I'm Going To Do Now"

[what I should'a done then]
3-4-13
Song

I'm going to do now, what I should'a done then
I guess I'm old enough, to know where I've been

to know where to go, and what not to do again
so I'm going to do now – – what I should'a done then

I might sing, a song or two, or even write a book
I'd take a fishing trip, if I could bait my hook

or maybe learn to fly, and try not to crash
sail around the world – – if I can get the cash

yeah there's a lot of things, I've been meaning to do
I thought I'd take a little time, to write down a few

well I might go to Vegas, just to take a chance
but I'd probably end up, at the Bunny Ranch

that's not a good thing, for a man of my age
too many blue pills, might turn my last page

I might go to Hawaii, check out the grass skirts
that shouldn't hurt me, all I can do is flirt

maybe go to Korea, get an Asian massage
if they put me in a sauna, I'd be blinded by the Mirage

it's easy to tell, as my mind begins to wander
just what kind of spell, this world's got me under

but I'm not givin in, and I'm not gonna crumble
I'll just hang around the house, and learn how to mumble
after all, it might seem a little sad
to die for something, I already had

yeah, I was going to do now, what I should've done then
but these are things I've done, and places I've been

and I do agree, it would be pretty sad
if I were to die for something, that I already had

so I ain't doin' it now, cause back then it was nice
and you can ruin your tobacco, if you chew it twice

so I'm not doing now what I should'a done then
and I swear <u>by thunder, this, is the end!!!</u>

"Citizens of----------------" [1st letter]

late--------- early
{or}
61-------------- 62

Dear citizens:
Before going into full detail of the purpose for this public appeal, I would like to make a few things very clear.
The reason for this letter is purely of my own personal concern in the matter, nobody asked me to express my feelings to the public.
Therefore, I request that you, the people of ------- and surrounding areas, if after reading this letter you find there
is no truth or meaning, only concern without merit, please regard it as a rude interruption in the line of public reading material and a waste of space in the newspaper, thank you.

Now, as most of you good people know, or if you don't I will do my best to make you aware of the fact that we have, in-------------- and its surrounding communities, approximately seven hundred youths between the age of twelve and twenty. We have in this same area approximately three thousand adults. Yet in comparison to the youth, the adults have six times as many clubs and other organizations to entertain themselves and be entertained at. Outside of beer joints and pool halls, the youth, or should I say your youth, have but two or three places to find entertainment. The question is, what are you going to do about it? Do you want your children to go to the beer halls for their entertainment? They will you know, and for this reason, there is not enough of what it takes in these three places to keep them occupied. Even if there were, if just one third of the youth would go to these places on the same night they would be hanging out the window. This would be from lack of space.

I sincerely believe that the majority of you are concerned with the welfare and benefit of your youth. But still, we have the question, are you concerned enough about their future to do something for them now?

There are a few of our citizens that look at this particular matter with a closed mind. These persons will say, the trouble with these kids today is that they already have too much to do. When I was a kid we didn't have one fourth the things to do these kids have now. I don't know about you but personally I am very familiar with this line. I should be, I've heard it from time I was fourteen.

The point I am trying to make is this. The purpose of this proposal is for the present and the future not the past.

We are living in a progressive and ever changing country. Thirty years ago we had no Sputnik's, no rockets no guided missiles, and only 48 states. Nor did we have all of the modern machines and household utilities that we have today. Therefore, the youth then had more chores, more work to do to occupy their time.

It all adds up to this, when people live in a country that is continuously changing and progressing, it is just natural for them to change and progress with it. As a matter of fact, I believe it is to a certain extent expected. For instance, how would you feel about living in this advancing age and having to drive an automobile that was manufactured in the 20s. It is easy to refer to examples or make an analogy that would fit in this particular case. However, it is my contention this would only be serving as a detriment to the objective.

As you know, and if you will admit it. You, the people living in this referred to area, have changed along with the fashions and the styles of time. Then you should admit too, and go along with me in believing that the youth of this said community should be allowed to change with the times.

Now, I believe, it is time to reach the heart of my proposal. You men of this area, when you wanted a country club, it didn't take you forever to get it. And that is good. It is certainly both an improvement and a change. But don't you believe that a community building, or Civic Center, would also be a great improvement, and a great change in many ways?

I am not saying it would keep all the youth off the streets and out of beer halls. At least it would give them a sense of being and belonging. They would know also, they would have a place to go and be sure of the right kind of amusement, instead of out looking for, and perhaps finding and taking the first type of entertainment that comes along.

They are your children, and will be one day, if not already, a part of your future. Each and every one of you are responsible for them, in one way or another.

So my proposal is this. That you, the citizens of this particular area take it upon yourself to see that your children - your grandchildren -your nephew- your niece, or whatever relation they may be, have a decent and proper place to go where they can find the right kind of amusement.

I wish to thank each one of you, who read this letter, for your valuable time and sincerely hope it starts you thinking.

Very truly yours
Keith Vance

"The "Ole" Red Creek Store"

11-23-2000
{song}

oh the "ole" Red Creek store isn't there anymore.
no the "ole" Red Creek store isn't there anymore

A new building stands on that same plot of land
but the "ole" Red Creek store isn't there anymore
it's not there anymore

the friends that I had when I was a lad
have somehow passed through life's door
through memories I sing of these beautiful things
but the "ole" Red Creek store isn't there anymore

from the old nursery bottom to the Jenningston
church, Many nights it's been walked alone

for the love of his life will soon be his wife
and he will claim her for his own

from hotels, and sleigh bells, night dreams and cocktails,
as we fall to life's lingering lure

we all leave behind the importance of time
and the "ole" Red Creek store isn't there anymore
it's not there anymore

through the passing of time with a mellowing
mind peace and tranquility we find

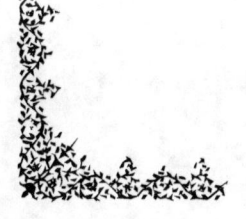

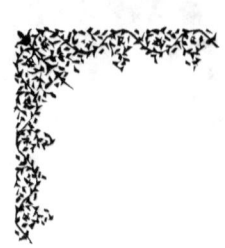

nothing stays the same
when we cross that plain

and the "ole" Red Creek store
isn't there anymore
take the Jenningston trail
to the jitney by rail

from ridge to ridge
on the old swinging bridge

though scarcely secured
the river we'd ford

but the "ole" Red Creek store
isn't there anymore
so shakily creaking
and made out of board

no the "ole" Red Creek
it's not there anymore

with church bells,
fire bells and dinner bells sure

but the "ole" Red Creek store
isn't there anymore

for a miseried mind
stop at Bonners for shine

it will help you decline
from the passing of time

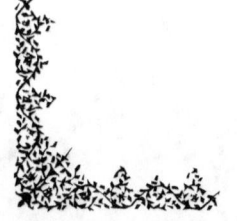

still the "ole" Red Creek store
won't be there like before
it's not there anymore

oh there's Black-fork, Maple-fork
pitch-fork and table-fork

but the "ole" Red Creek store
isn't there anymore

not many, if any, of these things are here
very few of these things are here anymore

with progress to excess and increasing access
left few of these beautiful things here anymore

and that "ole" Red Creek store isn't here anymore
no the "ole" Red Creek store isn't here anymore
it's not here anymore

"A Rose For Mother"

3-17-61

to you my dearest mother
a present I do bear

hold still now while I place
it among those silver hairs

it is indeed a beauty,
'twas the first I found this year

that's why I brought it
straight to you, my mother dear

it is the first to come about
by a belated breath of spring

like you, mother dearest, are first
with me, in thoughts and everything

though it is of much beauty
it could never ever compare
with you my lovely lady
and your tender loving care

for the sight of you, oh mother dear
turns night to brightest day
yet in just a few short hours
this flower wilts away

'tis what separates you mother
while your love and beauty goes on
as for this little flower, by day's
end, it's beauty will be gone

it is so very wonderful mother
how your beauty grows and grows

it holds a lot in common,
with that, of the un-plucked rose

I should like to give you thousands

but I have only found just one
and with it I give to you
a rose, from your loving son

"A Spark Of Love"

5-16-61

I can feel a violent yearning
deep within my heart

I can hear birds singing
to each other far apart

somewhere I see a lighthouse tower
on a little plot of land

then I'm overcome by love's power
from the gentle touching of your hand

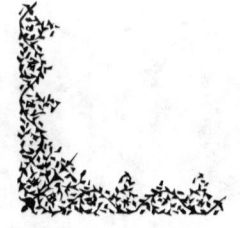

while above the heavens glitter
filled with stars so very bright

in the cool night breeze you shiver
as you hold me oh so tight

we ask each other, could this be
the opening of love's gate

or maybe we should wait and see
what's in the hands of fate

"Phantom Lover"

5-16-62

"____" my dear, I adore thee
though silent I must remain

your beauty I welcome before me
as the flowers are welcomed by spring

your smile is brighter than sunshine
brought about by the month of July

thy face, is lovely like Springtime
when the robins, so cheerfully fly

combine all the wonders of nature
and compare them my lady to you

heaven would lose all its thunder
for such injustice, to you is undue

now in closing, "___", 'tis advice I do bear

and this message to thee I must give

when approached by a stranger beware,
or in your world that stranger, forever, will live

miles and years, between us may come
I shall always, remember your touch

those timeless moments, made memories from
when we loved each other so much

"Loving You Is What I Do"

11-27-96

I'll tell you a secret
I hope you know is true
loving you is the last thing
that I will ever do

loving you is so easy
and your love lasts so long
your love leaves me weak
but gives me strength to go on

I know you don't understand it
and you may think, it's a lie
but loving you is what I do
until the day I die

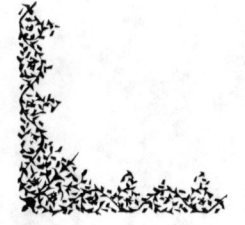

Eighteen Years And Eighteen Roses

12-22-63

one lovely rose
for each wonderful year

it has taken nature
to complete a flower so dear

one who's beauty far surpasses
that of the yellow Rose

unlike that rose, don't whither
instead more beautiful doth grow

eighteen years, and eighteen lovely yellow roses
I could not find a gift more complete

to give the one who introduced me
to the true meaning of defeat

the last five roses caressed tightly
by a ribbon you have found

and so the past five years with you
around my heart are just as tightly bound

to me you were a "God"-send
I should have treated you as such

now I think of the wrongs I've done
you've suffered much too much

so if you should ever need someone
if there's anything I can do

you need not ask, just say hello
and I'll be right there with you

although my love was never true
as are the heavens above

in my own way I truly give
to you, my undying love

"Pure"
2-9-63

you my dear I could describe
with many many words

though I may uncover some
this world has not yet heard

you are kind and so considerate
with a heart that's filled with love

I feel truly safe in saying
you descended from above

through all your radiant beauty
a friendliness does show

'tis as though you wish to say
hello, hello, hello

with every little smile you give
more beauty does uncover

which confirms my true belief,
of life, you are a lover

"Not That I Care For Her"

1962-63
{song}

she's the bloom, the pretty blossom
of a rose that blooms so fair

she's got little yellow ribbons
running through her pretty hair

she's a memory of a romance
that has grown apart

not that I care for her
but that she's got my heart

I once loved her as a blessing
I gave her all my love

she treated me as someone
sent from up above

then somehow I grew unfaithful
and our love just fell apart

not that I care for her
but that she's got my heart

I betrayed her yellow ribbons
and put them in my past

then suddenly I realized
that time was moving fast

she offered me one more chance
to make another start

not that I care for her
but that she's got my heart

now her love is for another
her love for me has grown cold

sometimes I sit and wonder
if that's why I'm growing old

how I wish I had taken her offer
and made a brand-new start

not that I care for her
but that she's got my heart

"Lady Love"
5-16-66

she must be an Angel straight from heaven
for her eyes hold the beauty of the sky

but her tempting, teasing ways, drive me crazy
and I know that I will love her until I die

she leaves me feeling, oh – so good
loving me, like no other could

she'll keep pleasing me this way
though she knows, I know, she can't stay

she always make's sure I'm satisfied
so I'll wait until she is gone, before I cry

there is not one man, in this whole world
who has the right, to hold this girl
so she chooses me, with many others
and though we know, we're not her lovers

these things about her, we understand
but it hurts to know, I'm not the only man

"Citizens of------------"

letter--#
2 10-8-62

Well now, it has been quite some time since I submitted my last letter to you. But after all, one must face the situation this way. We must not think back, because we realize the enormous amount of progress we have made in the fulfilling of this particular project's expectations

Ah yes, we must indeed be proud of our accomplishments. One in particular of which I believe we are succeeding in setting a new record for the arresting young people.

Is this really the right way? Destroy them, for the more we destroy and drive away, the fewer we have to contend with and provide for. ***We can do for ourselves, what we won't do for them.

And what are they doing here? I am quite positive they did not ask to be born.

Someone told me, the older people get, the wiser they get. However, I believe in this particular environment we might say, the older the majority of the people get, the more miserly they become.

And this, my money loving friends, is true. The almighty dollar has come to be our idol. Throughout biblical history, we find people worshiping golden images. Still today, thousands of years later, we have a generation which is supposed to be advanced, and swarming savagely, towards the intellectuals. Yet the intelligent people of today are idolizing a <u>flimsy little green colored piece of paper</u>, which does not even come close in equation, to the value of our youth.

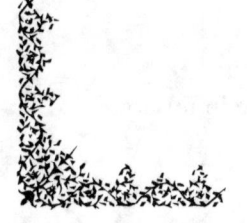

Maybe we are worshiping it for a different purpose. It could be we are planning on taking it with us when we die. What for, they won't be selling ice water in hell, and we surely won't need it in heaven.

At any rate, I shall leave you with these questions. When you look back to your children or your grandchildren ask yourself--these questions.
Shall we destroy them?
Shall we drive them away?
Should we do for ourselves, and not for them, are they too good to play with other children – – should we provide for them the social, and recreational activities they need???

Thank you,
very truly yours

Keith Vance

"Love Questions" #1

{at age 19}
9-13-61

if you lose your sweetheart for some little thing
you say or do
then suddenly you realize she knew you were
untrue
what will you do, will you run to her with a promise to be true
or will you turn your back and leave her in your past
although you realize for her your love will forever last
so tell me, please tell me, what would you
do
if something like this were to happen to
you
if someday her love you crave, would you live your life in misery

or would your lonely yearning heart, die in
agony
we know they say hearts heal
with time
but memories of broken dreams never
leave your mind

comp—52 years later

"Pay No Mind"

2-11-63
{song}

pay no mind to what I've said, just make-believe that I am dead
don't let it get to you, or you'll be doing the things I do
now listen to what I say, for I know how I got this way

{don't pay me no mind – forget about me} – {guitar run}

she told me the same thing that I am telling you
oh, how much I loved her, it broke my heart in two
she said, "honey I'm sorry but tonight we are through
that's the way it is, and that's the way it's gotta be
so darlin', please forget about me"

don't pay me no mind – forget about me

but I wasn't able to, my feelings took their part
for she held the only key, that could unlock my heart
we all learn by doing so I tried hard to forget
I've tried everything but it has happened yet

don't pay me no mind – forget about me – {guitar run}

Lord knows I miss that girl and it's so plain to see
I guess I've always known she was the only one for me
though I didn't treat her right, I could never be true
and my dear be careful, or the same thing could happen to you
so darlin' please, forget about me

pay no mind to what I said, just make-believe that I am dead
don't let it get to you, or you'll be doing the things I do
now listen to what I say, for I know how I got this way
don't pay me no mind, forget about me
yes darlin' please, forget about me

"Why Can't It Be Me"

2-14-62
Song

you want somebody to take care of you
someone who can make all your dreams come true

he'll have to be with you both night and day
be around when he's needed to do what you say

I have tried so hard, your heart to please
but your heart is blind, or just won't see
oh why, can't it be me

you want somebody to love you any-time
the lovin' mood comes to your mind

either you don't realize, or just don't care
what you're doing to my heart, is so unfair

please give me a sign, so I can find the key
to unlock your heart, and let you see
oh why, can't it be me

it seems the more I try to talk, the less you listen
what it takes to make you happy, is what I'm missing

if you would give me a chance to change your mind
I could make you want to leave the others behind

let me prove to you that I have what you need
and once and for all we can both agree
there is no reason [why, it can't be me]

"Small Wonder"

12-15-63

her hair is as red as the sunset, her eyes are as blue as the sky
her skin soft and fair as an Angel's, small wonder, in heaven am I
her smile bright and warm as the sunshine, her voice perfection, no less
her actions speak high with favor, small wonder, I love her I guess
her lips are much sweeter than honey, her body so soft to the touch
her kiss sets my heart all a flutter, small wonder, she thrills me so much
her beauty consumes all the flowers, her heart filled with love so divine
her I will love as long as a lifetime, small wonder, i'm happy she's mine

"A Poet-Or-Writers Nightmare"
3-4-14

I had the words and lines, to a song I'll never know.
I reckon it will have to wait, for memory to show
you gotta have a pen and paper, recorder or a phone
lost thoughts are a mental cost, as the past has shown
it could have been a memory of a lover and a child
or it might have been a picture that made you smile
to not remember a line important at the time
to a writer is committing the ultimate crime
have your pen and paper ready and write it down
you never know if that thought will come back around
and when you lose it, it isn't even a memory
the agony of loss will never let you be
so let this serve as a reminder to always be prepared don't let your
thoughts go silent, let the world know you care!!!

Dirty Black Coal

{or}
[poor folks' gold]
1979
{song}

my dad, he was a miner, and his heart was, until he died.
Lord knows – that he – had been mashed – up – – 10 or 15 times.
At the bottom – – of those lonesome – –"ole" mines.
Way – way down – in those dirty – – coal – – mines.
No – one knew-or-understood-, why he – – would go – – back in.
There was something – – deep – – down in the mines, he thought more
of than a friend. Guess the mines – were his – – – best friend – –.
Yes the mines, were his best friend.
The mines – – will – give – – you a fever –,
and it – – will steal – – your – soul.
And you – – will spend – – the rest – – – of –
your – life – – – diggin' – that – dirty – – –
black – coal. Just – diggin' – – that – dirty – black – coal. Chorus
[comes in quickly after coal]--- and faster!
dirty black coal, dirty black coal, some people call it,
"poor folks' gold".
Dirty black:, dirty black coal ---aw – – but – –
it's – – just – – like – the devil,
it destroys – – your – – soul.

{Same verse faster beat}
now my daddy was a miner and he was until he died
"lawd" he's been mashed – up 10 or 15 times
I could never understand why he'd go back in
something deep down in the mines
he thinks more of than a friend
and once you get it deep under your skin
you might as well give up, because you're already kin

yeah, your kin to the groundhog and the mole
you'll spend the rest of your days, diggin' dirty black coal
Chorus
he never thought about quittin' cause he couldn't if he tried
there was something in the mines that filled him up inside
the dust and the gas was food for his soul
he just kept – a – diggin' that dirty black coal

[possible music run to reflect mining simulation]
they brought him out for the last time in "71"
it was hard to believe that his mining days were done
for 29 years he took that bucket for a ride
then "God" saw fit to bring him out alive
yes, "God" saw a good man, and brought him out alive
end with chorus
[start the same, then, drag out the last line]

"Staten Island Blues"

2-11-71
{song}

a story about a guy
a small-town country boy
he said, "I'm going to the city
just to listen to the noise"

now he left the peace and quiet
of that little mountain state
when he got to Staten Island
it was getting kind of late

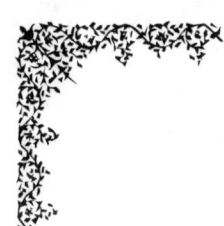

he's got the Staten Island blues
couldn't find a place to stay
and that West Virginia bed
Lord, is a long, long way

now let me have my mountains
you can have your city lights
and I'll take a country girl
every single night

now the city girl, she's fine
cause she knows just what to do
but I ain't found a single one
to kick these Staten Island blues

I got the Staten Island blues
I sure want to leave this town
I'm going back to the country
so's I can lay my body down
– a – yodel – lay – hey – he – he – he

now I came to Staten Island,
just to buy myself a car
a broken down old taxicab
that probably won't go far

I got the Staten Island blues
and it's raining all over me
that "ole" New York rain is cold
lawd--lawd, it's as cold as it can be

oh, I'm stuck in Staten Island traffic
and I ain't got no place to go
Lord, when I get back to those mountains
I swear, I ain't gonna leave no more

yeah – – got the Staten Island blues
ya know they make me want to run
run right back to West Virginia
where I can have my kind-a-fun

oh those Staten Island blues
they can make a man so sad
when you're homesick for the hills
and you need a mountain woman bad

yeah now, the Staten island blues
– a – yodel – lay – hey – he – he – he!!!

"Barefoot And Pregnant"

1970's
{song}

Chorus
Keep'em barefoot and pregnant and home with the kids
no one did it better than my daddy did
twenty years later the father of nine
no one did it better than that daddy of mine

keep them warm in the winter so they don't catch a cold
and branded in the summer so you know they're at home
it's an old country theory proved time after time
and no one did it better than that daddy of mine

{piano run}
for a home to be happy it needs kids and a wife and if
the wife's always pregnant she'll be there for life
it's fun growing up in a house full of kids
and our house was full of what my daddy did
[end with chorus]
keep'em barefoot and pregnant and home with the kids
no one did it better than my daddy did
twenty years later the father of nine
no one did it better than that daddy of mine

"Keep The Lid On The Bottle"

11-23-12
[song]

{begin with chorus}

daddy please keep the lid on the bottle
and don't let out those nasty "ole" snakes
cause they start crawling up and down you
every time you get the shakes
and it scares me so I think my heart will break
so daddy tighten up the lid on the bottle
and keep those "ole" snakes away from me
I'll love you just as much, without that creepy touch
and when you're drinking, those snakes won't let me be
now you promise every day you're going to quit
I reckon you ain't got around to it yet
I'm gonna buy you a bottle-top-stopper, and keep it under lock and key
maybe that will keep them snakes away from me
when we got married you promised me the moon
but you stopped at a bar along the way

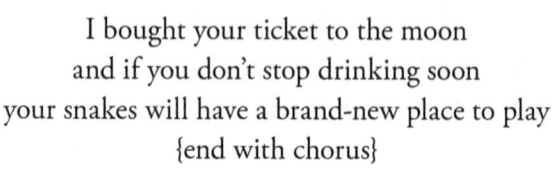

I bought your ticket to the moon
and if you don't stop drinking soon
your snakes will have a brand-new place to play
{end with chorus}

"A Dollar A Shot"

1-14-12

she was an old lady, a good friend of mine
she emptied her bottles one shot at a time
down a dark alley, first door on the right
she's got Jack and Jim for sale every night
it don't cost much, just a dollar shot
no cause to complain, it is what you got
it may be half water, but it's a dollar shot
she's open all night, put your money in the slot
and she'll keep you happy for a dollar a shot
well if she knows you you know what she's got
you might get lucky and sleep on her cott
but there ain't nothing free, it's still a dollar shot
at four in the morning there is no coffee pot
she's still pouring Jack for a dollar a shot

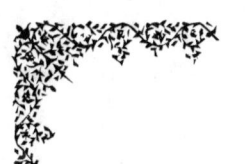

"Pen And Phone"

3-28-14
Song

well I got a pen, and baby I got a phone
give me your number, I can call you at home
if you don't answer, I'll be all alone
I'll just buy a bottle, and write a country song
I know you're busy, and you got to be goin'
but honey I got a pen, and I've got a phone
if you've got a little time, I don't need a lot
I'll call you up, and be "Johnny on the spot"
now a lady like you, should never be alone
and honey, I got a pen, and I've got a phone
I could find a thousand ways, to turn you loose
to stay away from me, would be physical abuse
I'd like to lay you down, on a satin sheet
and tell you my life story, starting with your feet
baby give me a chance, to get you alone
I'd find a million ways, to make you moan
so if you could spare me, just a little bit of time
I'd try to convince you, you want to be mine
I'd be your "doggie", if you throw me a bone
we could saddle up, the "ole strawberry roan
you know a lady like you, shouldn't be alone
and baby I got a pen, and I got a phone

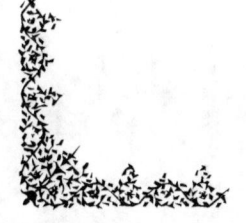

"The Days Of Poe"
11-4-11

I wish I had been living, back in the days of Poe
he had it oh so easy, don't you know

yeah they all had it easy way back then
it was in a time when the dictionary was a friend

"ole" Daniel Webster didn't have to look
he had plenty of words to fill his book

yes they all had it easy way back then
they could write a poem or book on a whim

all of words had not been used
the clichés were un-abused

now it seems everyone's a writer
although poets are much quieter

I guess being a writer, is a place to start
while poetry seems like a lost art

me, I like poetry and writing
sometimes my words come out fighting

they end up scrambled on the pages
maybe lost forever through the ages

I rearrange them to find meaning
and the dictionary leaves me screaming

my words are gone, how can this end
yes they all had it easy way back then

their dictionary was a bottle
not a massive verbiage throttle

how great he be, with his bottle better
would help him write, an endless letter

his vocabulary just seemed to overflow
I wish I had lived, in the days of Edgar Allen Poe

"Oh Virginia"

9-27-12
{song}

chorus
oh Virginia, you're my comfort if I cry
oh Virginia, would you hold me when I die
oh Virginia, you're so much a part of me
oh Virginia, you're the very heart of me
oh Virginia, there's no place I'd rather be
oh Virginia, than in your soil, through-out eternity

there's a little wide spot in the road
when you cross the Virginia state line
you can stop-- your car, and kiss the ground
or do whatever comes to mind
it's different air your breathing
and diff--er--ent scenery too
every now and then you can see, that "ole" rebel flag
flying with the red white and blue

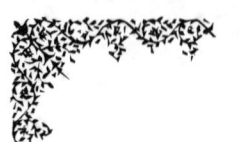

chorus
so many of our founding fathers
are still watching over you
and I know they're up there smiling
or at least that's what I would do
I am so proudly from you-- Virginia
you are the substance of this land
from oceanfront to mountaintop
your beauty is so grand
chorus
I speak to you as to my mother
for I was once your native son
I shall return to you-- Virginia
before my life on earth is done
extend to me a mother's welcome
when we Virginia- are as one
please cradle me oh-- my --Virginia
and warm me with your sun
or
[in your valleys, of the sun}
and so Virginia, you are my comfort

just hold me once more, when I die
I'll be the soil, spread through your heart-land
until we reach, our home on high!!!

"My Friend, Mr. Cho"

3-1-14

I was working in my garden, late spring of eighty-one
I saw my neighbor doing the same, his looked more like fun

to satisfy my curiosity, I walked across the yard
his soil seemed soft and smooth, where mine was kind of hard

he worked very diligently, and elevated every row
I introduced myself to him, he said, "hi – hello, I am Mr. Cho"

then Mrs. Cho called us in, to enjoy tea she had prepared
we talked about Korea and their business over there

they just moved here from Korea, not much English did they know
so together they explained to me, the elevated rows

they make a pretty picture, and is more fun to watch it grow
he bought the house next door, and became my good friend,
Mr. Cho

throughout the years, our friendship grew
he was like a brother I never knew

my life certainly had its ups and downs
but Mr. Cho was always around

in both our lives, we enjoyed success
and both our lives, "God" did bless

he in his right, and I in mine
we understood, our perfect rhyme

if I were he, and he were me
'twould be the same, for all to see

we were both blessed, with "God's" great love
and brother'd by, the one above

in my life, since our first meet
not one day goes by, my prayers don't seek

to protect and bless, the one I know
will always be, my Good Friend, "Mr. Cho"!!!

"For Tam"

4-14-11

[song]

you've been hurting me so-- long
that all my love for you is-- gone
and you just keep on keeping on—keepin' on doing
what you do – when you know it's wrong
if you don't love me – let me know – or let me go
cause I don't have what I want with you no more
that's been missin'-since we stopped kissin'
I can't remember the l-a-s-t time
you drove me out of my mind
in a good way
save your sorry – lame excuses – for your own kind – – on another day
yeah take what you've got and go
cause I don't have what I want with you no more
no I won't be grievin' as your leavin'
I want you to know – that you'll be pleasin'-me

so make yourself at home – on an out-of-town train
I hope that you and your new – love – get caught in the rain
and have stormy – weather– together – forever
"Tam"

"To Danielle"

11-20-10
{song}

Danielle, your swell
and you know that I can tell
because you do the things you do – – so well
Dan--ielle
it only takes one look
you're like a storybook
and all the while
you've got that Texas smile
a little southern belle
and anyone can tell
oh-- you wear it well
little cow-girl Queen
the best I've ever seen
you are any – – young man's dream
how many feelings fell
f-o-r-Dan-ielle
oh Danielle-- you're like the ring of a bell
or an ech--oing yell
repeating everything you tell
Dan-ielle
with every step you take
you cause a heart-land quake
another bronc to break
another world to shake

oh—my—Dan-ielle
your ship-- will surely sail
but not just another--leaf in a gale
is-- Danielle

"To Kristeen"

4-2-14

I hope the years are kind to you
as rightfully they should

for every time I think of you
it's always something good

I knew someday you'd find the one
that you could not turn down

I hope he's worthy of the prize
of who's heart he's holding now

I may or may not know him
but I wish you both the best

regardless of who, if I were to choose
they could never pass the test

these are just thoughts of how I feel
they're not important to the rest

just so you know, I always thought
you deserved better than the best
congratulations

"Father Time"

7-13-2000
[the poem]

I thought I'd left you far behind
that old man named father time
before I know I'll be going blind
father time you're no friend of mine

I can't see to read with my elbow bent
I thought I saw her coming but there she went
oh gee there goes my knee
father times catching up with me
now here I am at fifty-eight
I thought I was early but I'm runnin' late
it's time to sit back and relax
but when I do I have to face facts

when I was thirty-four I weighed 155
I could party all night and still be alive
now I'm fifty-eight and running late
it takes me all night long to clean my plate

I always wondered just where you'd be
you're the ugliest thing that I can't see
you have cut out all my good sunshine
so goodbye to you "ole" father time

"Father Time"

7-13-2000
[song style]

well I thought I'd left you far behind
that old man named "father time"
father – time you're no friend of mine
hey father – time you're no friend – a – mine
before I know, I'll be going blind
father – time, you're no friend – a – mi---n-e
I can't see to read with my elbow bent
I thought I saw her coming, but there she went
father – time you're no friend of mine
hey father – time you're no friend – a – mine
oh gee, there goes my knee
father – time's catchin' up with me
father – ti-yi-yime, you're no frie—nd of mi--ne
now here I am at fifty eight
I thought it was early but I'm runnin' late
father– time, you're no friend of mine
hey father – time, you're no friend – a – mine
it's time to sit back and relax
but when I do I have to face facts
father – time, you're no friend of mine
hey father – time, you're no friend – a – mine
yeah before I know, I'll be going blind
father – time, you're no friend of mine
hey father – time you're no friend – a – mine
father –ti-yi-yime, you're no friend – a –mi---ne

oh gee there goes my knee
father time's catchin' up with me
when I was thirty - four I weighed 155
I could party all night and still be alive
father – time, aaww, you're no friend of mine
hey father – time, you're no friend – a – mine
now I'm fifty - eight and a runnin' late
it takes me all night long just to clean my plate
O father – time, you're no friend of mine
hey father – time you're no friend – a – mine
father –ti-yi-yi-yi-yime
you ain't no dad – blamed friend – a – mi-i-ine
well I always wondered, just where you'd be
you're the ugliest person that I can't see
oh gee there goes my knee
father time's sneakin' up on me
father – time, you're no friend of mine
hey father – time, you're no friend – a – mine
you done cut out all my g-o-od sunshine
so goodbye – – father time
[talk partly]---get on outta here
I'm going back to the way it was
get me some transplants – a new hair – do
a face – lift or two, then sc---r-e-w you
father time – – you're no friend of mine
yeah I always wondered where you'd be
you are the UGGGLIEST person I never did see
gooood-bye faather time!!!

"Stacey My Bartending Lady"

1998
{song}

Oh, – – – Stacey my bartending lady, I keep
thinking you might be a maybe;
then I remember you are someone else's baby, Stacey my bartending lady;

she keeps a close watch on this check of mine,
sometimes I think that beer just costs a dime;
And she never charges me for overtime,
{she's so fine, I'm there all the time}

sometimes I think that she don't even care, then she
lets me know she always knows I'm there;
and when my check comes it's so much more than fair,
{she's so fine, I'm there all the time}

aw, – – – Stacey my bartending lady,
Lord knows you might be a maybe ;
if it weren't that you were someone else's baby,
oh Stacey – – my bartending lady;

on – a – Wednesday I head on up to Outback,
cause Stacey is up there tending bar;
on – a – Thursday I head right back to Outback,
I had one too many and I can't drive my car;

oh – – – Stacey my bartending lady, by this time I know you're maybe
and I don't care if you're someone else's baby,
cause Stacey your my bartending lady;

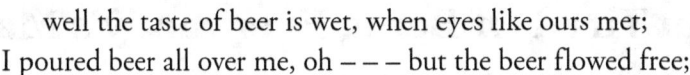

well the taste of beer is wet, when eyes like ours met;
I poured beer all over me, oh – – – but the beer flowed free;

I went to the Outback bar tonight, I had one too many and I got tight;
{and I tried, tried, tried – tried to hide – tried to hide}

when I stood up to head for the door, it was all I
could do to keep my knees off the floor;
{but I tried, tried, tried – tried to hide – tried to hide}

oh – – – Stacey my bartending lady, you are no longer a maybe;
cause in my mind you are my baby, Stacey my bartending lady;

now you wonder why I'm always wearing black, it's
because you're gone and you are not coming back;
until you're at that bar and in my sight, they'll
never ever see me dressed in white;

oh – – – Stacey my bartending lady, I keep
thinking you might be a maybe;
but in reality you are someone else's baby, aw – –
but, Stacey you 're my bartending lady"

I'm Tired Of Being Everybody's Man

6-20-80
{song}

chorus

well I'll smoke a little dope if I want to
and I'll drink a lot of beer every time I can
I'm gonna live my life the way it feels good
cause I'm tired of being everybody's man

now the law says you gotta do things this way
and my wife sometimes won't let me be

when will they understand I am a freeborn man
and my whole life belongs to me

way back when I was a boy
all my folks had my life planned
but it came together late now I'm thirty eight
and by-god it's time I took a stand

so I'll, chorus

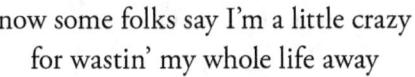

now some folks say I'm a little crazy
for wastin' my whole life away

if you think I'm a nut you can kiss my country butt
cause I don't give a damn what you say

and I'm gonna chorus

"To Keith"

2-21-80

Keith
thank you for letting me stay and sleep a while. I wish you could
have been sleeping with me, but since you couldn't, sleeping
in your bed is the closest I can get to sleeping with you!

I love you Keith, and I know I'll never love any other man.
To me, I am a part of you and you are a part of me. My love is so
strong so binding. In my mind life simply would not be without you.
Maybe it has something to do with the fact that I was
so young when I met you. You will always be the big, strong,
handsome, all-knowing man you have been to me since day one

I hope we can find it in us to be happy.
I really want to try I hope you do too.

displayed on a drawing of a heart,
with an arrow entering and exiting
----was----
love,
Donna

P. S. Hey sexy! Making love was beautiful last night!

In response to her own letter

maybe I should not have written the way I feel. May seem silly to you. I'm sure you could find someone to take my place now. Maybe I lost your love, after reading this, I read a couple things you wrote last May. Let me know how you really feel about me.

"To Donna"

11-11-78

I am your servant
I worship thee
my living demands your love
on the day I die
my heart will be full of love for you
your beauty will fill my eyes
for you are mine
and I am yours
together if it may be
apart if it must be

11-23-78

let me die as I lay dreaming
of a love that will not be
with a smile upon my face
as life from me I chase
while I still want there to be
a lifetime of you and me maybe with a little time
if I lose you I'll keep my mind

heart-mind-body-soul
you are what makes me whole
you're the beating of my heart
though I know someday we'll part
Donna, I will love you Always!!!
Keith

"For Karen"

5-4-14

for you this poem I have written
long past time for you for quittin'

you've lived for years with time and tears
and life preformed through hours of wear

the non-concern for love's true meaning
leaves only room for intervening

months and years the same "ole" thing
no solace does the future bring

with hope all gone for now it seems
life has portrayed our broken dreams

the children raised life's chores are done
you look towards the setting sun

I say to you, {you are the one}
now is the time to have some fun

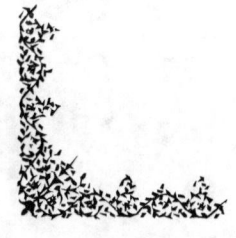

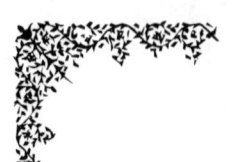

"Loves End"

4-5-14

relationships are, truth, trust, and love
we want to believe we have, all of the above
until that tragic day, life takes off its glove
no more belief, truth and trust we shove

what once was love has turned to hate
what we have now cannot equate
to what we thought, but much too late
we've turned the tide to clean the slate

for what, for why, results of lies
what now, forget the cringing cries
there is only left to say goodbye
alas, stand-by to watch love die

we have no-fault, we have no-blame
with no remorse, we feel no shame
we lived in love, and shared the same
divorce is now our claim to fame

we choose to part with days of yore
no memory's knock on our front door
'twas once good, 'tis now quite sore
hence love lives here, never-more

"Cheat River Bride"

8-12-11
{song}

I loved her and lost her and met my demise
while watching the Cheat River rise
yeah, watching the Cheat River rise
I remember the look in her eyes
and the last words she said as the water sped by
was I love you and I will till I die
oh – – – we watched that "ole" Cheat River rise
on the banks of the park, from daylight till dark
as the river got a higher we lost track of time
while watching the Cheat River rise
with no stars in the sky and no light to guide by
we watched the "ole" Cheat River rise
don't make love by the Cheat, if you can't see the water go by
that's how the Cheat got its name
the end's always the same
if you get too close you will die
and – – we watched that "ole" Cheat River rise
her hair was long – flowing in the water
it caught on a limb floating by
on her face the look of love lingered longer
as did the sparkle in her eyes
while watching the Cheat River rise
yeah – – we watched that "ole" Cheat River rise
with the Cheat at my feet
I dived in the deep
to save my lovely young bride
but the current was stronger than I
oh – – the current – much – stronger – than I
I pulled her body to mine
and there together we died

while watching the cheat River rise
oh – – together they died
while watching that "ole" Cheat River rise
and so goes the legend of the "Cheat River bride"
and they still watch that "ole" Cheat River rise
he and she – – oh – – still watch the "ole" Cheat River rise

{background music}
now Mama said kids don't go near the water
I went down to the river to watch the water roll by
o-o-o-o-h I am so lone--some-------
well they went down three times – – – stretch this part out
but they only came up twice – – – – – moaning low and sad
and now they're go –o-o-ne to watch that "ole" Cheat River rise

{background music through out this whole section}

you know, some folks say, that late at night,
if you are walking in the park,
and the moonlight is just right,
you can see two silhouettes sitting on the banks of the cheat,
arm in arm, holding hands, just watching the Cheat River rise
oooooooooooh--sooooo--looonesoome
{at the same time in the background}
{soft and low}
Mama said kids please don't go near the water

"Playing Love Games"
7-2-76

would you look at the rain – a – fallin'
just look at that rain – a – fallin'
plumb out – a – my mind and high on love
and I don't feel like bawlin'
baby I don't feel like bawlin'

would you look at the lightning
take a look at that lightning
plumb out – a – my mind baby high on love
and I don't feel like fighting
honey I don't feel like fighting

now listen to the thunder roar
just listen to the thunder roar
plumb out – a – my mind baby high on love
and now I'm headin' for the door
you see me headin' for the door

would you look at those trees – a – growing
just look how the trees are growing
plumb out – a – my mind and high on love
and I don't know where I'm – a – going
I don't have any way of knowing

do you ever count white lines on the road
try counting white lines on the road
plumb out – a – my mind baby high on love
just out here loosening up my load
you know I got a mighty heavy load

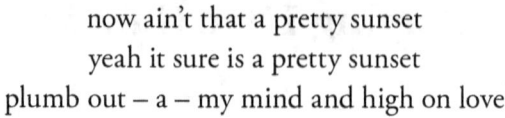

now ain't that a pretty sunset
yeah it sure is a pretty sunset
plumb out – a – my mind and high on love

and I haven't done anything yet
no I ain't done nothing yet

just look at that "ole" quarter – moon
would you look at that quarter – moon
plumb out – a – my mind and high on love
and you know I'm gonna get there soon
yeah baby I'll be home soon

we sure have a long road ahead
honey we got a long road ahead
plumb out – of – my mind baby high on love
and I am ready for the bed
baby we can work it out in bed

Dry Cleaning Route-Man Super-Star

[11-66 to 9-77 to 4-14]
[song]

they gave him his orders in Annandale Virginia
they said today you will run a different line

this is not your run but a driver didn't show
and you gotta bring it back on time

he looked at his boss and he looked at his load
then he looked at the falling snow

he said I don't know what you think I am
but I ain't no damn Dynamo

now it's a mighty rough road from McLean to Fairfax-at
the part where they are tearing up the road

and as he went flying by
he caught a glimpse of a thigh
and emptied his whole damn load
well there's a lot of pretty sights between McLean an
Fairfax-you can see them all along the way

now he was surely lookin'-his attention had been
tookin'-and no skid-marks were left that day

yes he was found there in the dirt
all wrapped up in a skirt
an strangled by a little pair of panties

all you route men wives should adjust your lives or
your husband will be seeking someone dainty

"To Mary Jane"

[date unknown]

hello, Mary Jane, are you working on my brain
or are you looking for my main vein
well keep right on working on what ever your working on
maybe you'll find a clue to help you get along
if you conquer my brain
you control my veins
they all go together
but what will you do
when they rebel on you
and you end up in stormy weather
Mary Jane, you got powers
that lasts through the hours
but when you leave, I don't have to take cold showers
not that you don't turn me on because you know you
do but when it's over, it's over and that includes you
now don't let me mislead you, and I would if I could
but you know in the long run, you and I are no good

"The One That Got Away"

date unknown

though my title fails her sorely
this lady fills that bill
I miss her so adoringly
her pleasures haunt me still
to quote the friends that envied me
"you should have imposed your will"
with respect for her desire of chastity
by her pleasured company I was thrilled
and so my memories yield a glowing
while I watched her body sway
with complete content of knowing
as through my dreams we play
she no longer lives in haunting
for she's the one that got away

"Visions Of A Girl"

5-17-61

in the mind of every boy there is a picture of a girl
the kind of girl he must have to set his heart a-whirl

what she looks like doesn't matter, if she's the one for him
you can bet your bottom dollar, he will treat her like a gem
who she is or where she comes from, to him it's all the same
and he will not be happy, until he changes her last name

what her name is doesn't matter, you can bet that he don't care
the only thing he wants to know, is what size wedding band she wears
I myself had my own visions of the girl I would wed
and I have finally found her, as so many others did
now that we're joined together, we'll remain that way for life
and when the gates of heaven open, we shall enter man – and – wife

"Such A Little Kingdom

3-16-63

'tis but forty acres of swampland, hidden in the Florida Everglades
far out of touch with civilization, populated by crocodiles and snakes
I am the King of such a kingdom, though its boundaries I've never seen
it must be a wild little kingdom, most likely searching for a Queen
you with me to rule this kingdom, 'twould be a lover's Paradise
you could turn the crocodiles into kittens, without smiling twice
as your beauty watches o'er, it would be delightful to abide
and rule this little kingdom, with you forever by my side

"I Am Looking" #2

9-14-62

I don't know where I'm going
I don't care where I've been

I know that I must find someone
on whom I can depend

I have to find a lady love
that wants to settle down

it may turn out to be a stranger
maybe a new friend I've found

she don't have to be a beauty queen
she just needs a heart that's true

to have the heart and soul for love
is when real-pure-beauty shows through

there must be something I can recognize
something that attracts my eye

that tells me I must hold her there
as soon as she walks by

should I be so lucky
I will take her by the hand

yes I will take my lady love
to see the preacher man!!!

"Hey Ruka"

5-16-12
{song}

hey Ruka, what you say we have some fun
h-e-y Ruka, ya know we're old enough that it won't hurt anyone
so what you say Ruka, let's have a little fun
now listen to me Ruka, ya know my idea of fun
might be a little different today, then it once was
but we're both older now, and there's not a whole lot we haven't done
so what you say Ruka, why don't we just have – a little fun
aw-what you say Ruka, we can drive around and
talk smack maybe throw in a little trash
it'll all be harmless, and it helps the time to pass
it would help make memories, and in life – good
mem--ories should be number one
so what – you say Ruka, think maybe we can just – have some fun
you're a real sweetheart, and baby you know it's true

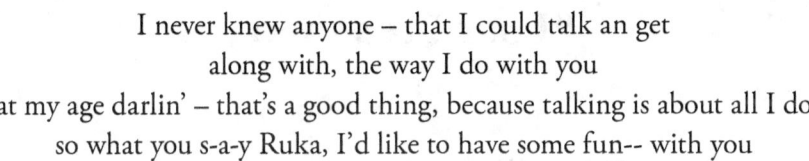

       I never knew anyone – that I could talk an get
along with, the way I do with you
at my age darlin' – that's a good thing, because talking is about all I do
so what you s-a-y Ruka, I'd like to have some fun-- with you

yes – I know you got – a boyfriend, and Ruka,
I could say I wish that wasn't true
life has taught me – to be a respecter of people cause
if you don't, it will all come back to you
---oh yeah, no-- matter what you do---
now you know – Ruka, I think he is a pretty nice guy
and when it's all said and done Ru-ka, we're not into hurting anyone
so – what – you – say Ruka, let's you and me have a little fun
one thing I know about you and me – Ruka, we were both born for fun
and I can tell the way you laugh Ruka, you
make up the better – half of fun
so what you say Ruka, now didn't we – have some fun
aw-- you know it girl, it's been a lot of fun

"Lost Treasure"

3-14-63

like the Robin seeks its mate in the early days of spring
same still the lucky lady with frequent glances to her ring
while 'tis small wonders of you that my desires do cling
I picture thee very lovely as Blackbeard must have seen
the certain beauty in a ship bearing treasures for the King
as he attempted boarding guns fired and swords clashed
both crews fighting fearlessly, alas, there came a splash
"aarrgh, it be our treasure," said Blackbeard, with a dash
through the Spanish Captain thrust his Cutlass with a smash
then straightaway to his own ship he made off like a flash
once away he shouted back though his vessel most unseen
"alright ye gallant Spaniards, I've a message for your King
tell him where his treasure be, and who put it there I mean
tell him his lust for riches I match with curses thou hast seen
aarrgh, to ye gutless seamen, mention Blackbeard to your King
whether it be on sea's bottom or in the belly of a whale
little good will it do us now while o'er its head we sail
for the beauty of this treasure never – more shall be unveiled"
'twas then the venture ended, from accountings in his log
though they were none the richer as the ship's bow split the fog
they headed homeward to rejoice through the silent dark of night
and in each pub a different story of how a treasure slipped from sight
same is with thee my lady love, I see my treasure in your eyes
a simple smile works wonders and your kisses hypnotize
yet one thing still puzzles me, should a pirate have the power
to pluck there from her master's hand such a lovely flower
aw 'tis true, I am a pirate, and you are the treasure I uncovered
Pirates take from the rich, even sometimes steal their lover
once I've captured you my dear, it will be my great conquest
I shall attempt no other for nothing's better than the best

"Side-Saddle"

9-9-70
Song

I'm ridin' side-saddle on a young mountain lion
it don't look like I'll ever sit

if I could get a-straddle, I wouldn't worry about
the saddle, slippin' just a little bit

I caught her on the fly, as she came by
didn't even take a second glance

I was in such a hurry, I had no time to worry
I almost got caught without my pants

she's just a little kitten with a mind of her own
slightly immature, just a cat half-grown

she's got a set of claws hanging on her paws
that just dig right into your mind

now I'm not complaining, I just keep thinking
I got myself one-of-a-kind

I really have to worry when she stops purring
then opens with a-cryin'-whine

she can send you flying, without even trying
and you're thinking it's the end of time

it's hard to catch your breath when you're facing
death, and don't know where you've been

then she slaps you with her paw, out comes the
claws, and she pulls you right back in

sometimes it's tough but I can't get enough
I'm addicted to her kitty-cat ways

maybe in a little while I'll get used to her style
and end up liking this place

it's those sudden groovy moves that leave me
breathless, and lets me know she wants to play

but it's so hard to straddle especially when the
saddle, keeps slipping every which-a-way

"I Just Can't Go"

11-21-70

what is this hold you have over me
that gnaws and tears at the heart in me

leading me to believe you really care
yet leaves a feeling of coldness there

from a warm part within the heart
that shows itself when we must part

then comes a cry I love you true
my heart desires to be with you

a burst of anger from deep within
not from the heart, 'tis pride again

stop this, what now my soul does cry
I feel I must leave but know not why

if I should leave because of pride
my fear is that one heart shall die

loneliness makes a dreadful sound
my tears flow freely to the ground

shared tears of pain, and tears of fear
tears of love lost through the years

fully clad with coat in hand
staring at the door I stand

surrounded suddenly with bliss
it is as though I feel her kiss
this cannot be, for in bed there
lay a goddess with angelic flare
but to approach this one so fair
would be a dream, an answered prayer

'tis when I truly understand
this one so fair is in command

now overwhelmed by charm I know
a picture spreads with heavens glow

how clear it is, I love you so
though try I must, I just can't go

"Lost"
10-3-71

in a manner of speaking it's a matter of time
in a matter of moments you'll be off my mind
it's a matter of loving and living alone
it's a matter of leaving a beautiful home

so bring on the wine and bring on the rum
I'm having a party and everyone come
let there be dancing singing and cheer
if we run out of rum we'll open a beer

doused in the rum and numbed by the wine
I'll leave my unhappiness and troubles behind
yes I know I'll return for the same thing to find
at least for the present I have a satisfied mind

so in a manner of speaking I'm doing just fine
in a matter of moments I'll be out of my mind

"I'd Venture To Say"

12-12-71

I'd venture to say you don't love me I'd venture to say that's the truth
I'd venture to say I'll find out some day, baby,
you've been loving somebody new
I'd venture to say you've been looking, for somebody
else
I'd venture to say you've been thinking of leaving
me by myself
I'd venture to say I'm heartbroken, think maybe
I spoke out of turn
for your adventurous ways my dear, someday
you're sure to get burned
adventure is part a of a journey we take
another part of that journey is love

they never could work well together
without a lot of help from above

adventure is always hanging around
where love is not often found

in adventure we look for excitement
with random, or sordid affairs

true love is filled with excitement
and overflowing with care

so be careful my dear, the places you go
have good reasons for what you do

there are some things you cannot forget
for they will always come back to you

life has a way of administering
the comings of around

and when it knocks on your door baby
it is an unforgettable sound

"It's Not Over For Me"

12-24-71

the judge signed the papers
and the lawyer's been paid

I have just made arrangements
for hiring a maid

she'll iron my shirts now
since you set me free

but it's not, oh no
it's not freedom for me

I still hold you, as I walk
these lonely halls, each day

to that big "ole" king-sized bed
where we used to play

these are visions these are memories
not taken by decree

and it's proof, yes it's full proof baby
it's not over for me

no it's not over for me
until I say so

you'll be right there in my memory
I may never let you go
I'll show you, what that "ole" judge
and all his papers mean to me

no honey, it's not over till I say
and that may never be

"My Chosen Memories"

12 – 26 – 71
{song}

you have turned away and wasted every time I tried
you put me off and led me on, till there is no more love inside
it's like I have been awakened from a million broken dreams
I don't love you but here you are, to take all and everything
{Chorus--#1}
and I kno---w someday you'll catch me crying
you will wo-n--der where you went wrong

but all this ti---me my love's been dying
I guess you--- left me lonesome too long

you could strip me of my pride, and all my
worldly gain

but I'd still have the memory, of a love that was unchained

through the pleasures of your company, your wish was my command

and to have walked this road with you, made me a wealthy man

{Chorus #2}

so I'll take--- my chosen memories to--- my world of make-believe
and you are not welcome there to ruin it for me
only good--times and laughter is all there'll be
no you can nev-er change my chosen memories

I have a picture in my mind of us the way it used to be
and you don't have to play the part you're there in memory
the dress you wear, you comb your hair, it lays upon your brow
in that same way I touched you then, is the way I'll touch you now
{end with chorus #2}

"Don't Feel Sorry For Me"

10 – 21 – 72

when you compare the way he kisses, and the
way he holds you tight
tell me darlin', do I ever enter into your dreams at night
when you compare the way he treats you, to the way you treated me
when you don't tell him where you're going,
do you think he's wanting to be free
when the secrets that he keeps from you, are of things you'll never know
do you compare the love you're getting, to the love that you let go
well it may-be for us it's over, and at last loves door has closed
your free of me, and the misery, that on you I have imposed

I have a new way of living, let me tell you how it is
each night I die a thousand deaths, from the memories of your kiss

you say you never heard me crying, as I do now in my sleep
the silence of a broken heart, is like watching robins weep
I think you have what you wanted, you afford no time for memory
but from what it seems that you have now darlin', don't feel sorry for me

"Someone You Never Knew"

12 – 20 – 72

it must be hard to miss someone
you never really had
who wasn't there to comfort you
when you needed him so bad

to miss someone who was always gone
it seems could never be
with this in mind I understand
why you do not miss me

but if somehow I could get through to you
and make you understand
the lacking of one's presence
does not make a lesser man

if I hadn't loved you dear I would not have worked those crazy hours
you were my bride and I desired to give you all within my powers

but it was you who forced the hand that struck
the final blow
I must accomplish something if not I fear
she'll go

so I set my goals my aim was high self-centered
I may be
but then no one is perfect to say the least
not me

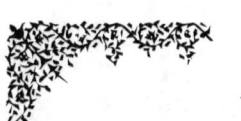

with half a dream behind us and the rest
still to come
suddenly you began to change it left me cold
and numb
bewildered by the loss of love that I fought hard
to keep
the end results of trying still haunts me
when I sleep

an accomplishment in which I take no pride
from lure
for without you dear should I be Caesar
I would still be poor

now with my hands tied to limited
compete
to win back the love that I have lost or clutch
the dagger of defeat

I can only hope and pray that "God", will let you see
the love and happiness you desire, still lives in me

"I'll Be Waiting Here At Home"

4-23-73

you thought your life had lost its meaning
so you left me for a brighter – better time
I know some day you'll feel the beaming
of a love you've kept hidden that was mine

I didn't know you were the party-girl kind
I don't blame you for doing what you've done
for to your needs of living I was blind
when you're finished I'll be waiting here at home

yes I'll be waiting here like I've always been
memories of love won't release the tie that binds
I've tried to leave a thousand times but I find then
I can't walk away and leave our love behind

so as your desires change and love brings you home
know that I will be here waiting when you come

"When You've Gone"

9-1-73
{song}

I can tell that you are leaving
cause I hear the teardrops fall

no one will know how much I'll miss you
and I guess you'll know least of all

chorus
oh it's sad to think about
it makes me feel so all alone
but when you leave I won't be lonesome
you'll take my heart with you when you've gone

now I can see the misery coming
yes I can feel the pain and woe

I can't believe our story's ending
and I am just holding on to let you go

no I won't spend my nights alone
I've got your memory's here at home

I'll make believe they are real
and loneli--ness I'll never feel
(end with chorus)
oh it's sad to think about
it makes me feel so all alone
but when you leave I won't be lonesome
you'll take my heart with you when you've gone

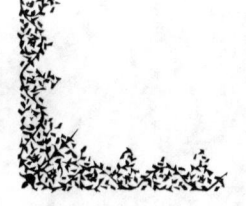

"What You Make Of Me"

2-3-75
{song}

(begin with chorus)
I can't be the one you want
and I can't hold you in your dreams
I'm only here for comfort dear to maybe make you see
that I can only be – what you make of me

well you say that you are waiting
for someone that you can't reach
and there will never be another
for to your heart he holds the key
and I am just a back – up lover
to help set your feelings free
and that's okay if you are sure
that is what you want from me

tenderness is all I see when I look into your eyes
makes me believe there is a message
you are trying to disguise
but now is when we're living
and only "God" can see
you know I love you – tell me darling
what will you make of me
(end with chorus)
I can't be the one you want
and I can't hold you in your dreams
I'm only here for comfort dear and to maybe make you see
that I can only be what – – you make of me

"All These Things"

3-28-78

if I gave you my heart to keep
would you be too shocked to speak
conversation is free and words are cheap
and some promises are hard to keep

if I gave you a baby
would you smile and say
maybe I'll be here
in a year – come what may

if I gave you a lifetime
of simple man and wife time
would you smile and say
I still love you today

if I gave you happiness and filled your life with bliss
if you felt faint with every kiss would you be content with this

if I gave you all these things
what would our tomorrow's bring
will tomorrow make a true heart sing
or could it be broken like a chain

nothing is a wedding ring
nowhere is a broken chain
what I know now is you are here
and I desire to keep you near

if we could tell tomorrow's find
should we spin it into rhyme

the mem-or-ies of countless springs
when we have now, all these things

we'll know soon enough what tomorrow brings

"She Sings Love Songs"

2-3-75
{song}

she sings love songs, sweet, sweet love songs
the sweetest love songs, I have ever heard
she sings love songs, sweet, sweet, sweet love songs
and she never, never ever, says a word
she walks into the room, and changes everything
oh, she changes everything
she walks into the room, and changes everything

and when she sings those love songs
those sweet, sweet love songs
she changes me, and makes me feel just like a king
by singing love songs, sweet, sweet love songs
yes she sings love songs, like I have never heard
she sings love songs, sweet, sweet, sweet love songs
and she never, never ever, says a word
she has dinner on the table, does laundry, and sweeps the floor
while singing love songs, sweet, sweet love songs
she irons my shirts, straightens my tie, and fixes so much more
just by singing love songs, sweet, sweet love songs
mmm-the sweetest love songs, I have ever heard
she sings love songs, sweet, sweet, sweet love songs
and she never, never ever, says a word
she pays the bills, goes to the bank, and no one ever tells her thanks
still she sings love songs, sweet, sweet love songs

she gets the car washed, and fills the tank
while singing love songs, sweet, sweet love songs
the sweetest love songs, I have ever heard
she sings love songs, sweet, sweet, sweet love songs
and she never, never ever, says a word
she is an artist, and she paints pictures of our life
while singing love songs, sweet, sweet love songs
she's my whole world, she is my wife
and she sings love songs, with every step she takes
she sings love songs, sweet, sweet love songs
without those love songs, I know my heart would break
oh, she sings love songs, sweet, sweet love songs
the sweetest love songs, I have ever heard
yes she sings love songs, sweet, sweet, sweet love songs
and she never, never ever, says a word

"Mixed Emotions"

12-15-71

I won't say that I don't love you, but the love I cannot see
I can't say I'll never leave you, we both know I want to be free
I guess I'm having mixed emotions about me

I cannot say that I am sorry, for the things I didn't do
I cannot say that I was happy, when you stayed to see me through
I guess I'm having mixed emotions about you

and sweetheart, I can't say I'm sorry I didn't answer every time you called
nor will I say I did not worry, about love's punch, as it did fall
I guess I'm having mixed emotions about it all

"Sadness"

5-9-78

to have you here with me
would be too much to ask

though you may not be in my future
I know I will always be in your past

the love that we shared
was a love that we dared

to adventure too long, much too long
now I feel so alone and far from home
home in your arms where I belong

sweetheart if you could see deep inside the heart of me
you would find a troubled soul in total misery

if there's one thing I will save
and take with me to my grave

I would give anything I own
if I were able to atone

and have the chance to do
one more memory with you

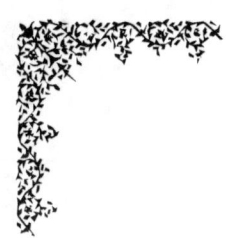

but oh how distant you seem
you're like an unfinished dream
that I reach for at night when I sleep

still the reason's unknown
for a love not full – grown
you're in my heart and that I will keep

"Mental Misery"

6-21-70

I wonder if somebody's waiting
whenever I leave home

I wonder if they go inside
to find you all alone

I wonder if they lust
for treasures I have known

I wonder if they seek
to please you when I'm gone

you tell me that you love
me that I am your only joy

you make me think I'm fantastic
America's first boy

no truth displayed there in your eyes
has another won my prize

and now my answer, so sadly soon revealed
not alone just lonely, in this mental-misery field

"No More"

8-5-76
Song

no more, O Lord, no more- I've traveled that road before
no more, O Lord, no more

I've been down that highway my last time
you can buy my experience for a dime
no more, O Lord, no more

that old road gets mighty rough
for a softhearted man it's a little tough
no more, O Lord, no more

now they say marriage is a sacred thing
but no more binding than a little gold ring
no more, O Lord, no more

I had a fine little woman pretty as could be
one day I went home - where could she be
no more, O Lord, no more

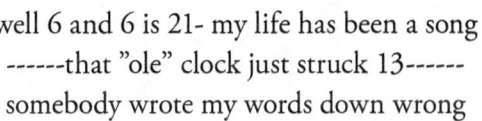

well 6 and 6 is 21- my life has been a song
------that "ole" clock just struck 13------
somebody wrote my words down wrong

no more, O Lord, no more- I've traveled that road before
no more, O Lord, no more

"You Had, Your Chance But You Blew It"

1975 – 76
{song}

(begin with chorus)
you had your chance but you blew it
you had me all wrapped up and you knew it
you rolled me up in a ball and then you threw it
baby you had your chance but you blew it

well, I always knew we'd get together again
but I just didn't know how long

now my heart is – a – achin' – breakin'
waitin' on the day you're comin' home

I'll tell you one thing and baby you know that I'll do it
commit "Hari--Kari" if I thought you came to stay
and I knew it

now I'm not saying you're ugly
but I can't stand the sight of your face

and I'm not trying to be rude
but the devil would be welcome in your place

every time you come around
you just run me in the ground

it makes me feel like a two-bit-piece
honey I hate lying I'd rather face dying

because you feel no pain
when you're deceased

(end with chorus)
you had your chance but you blew it
you had me all wrapped up and you knew it
you rolled me up in a ball and then you threw it
baby you had your chance but you blew it

"I Just Couldn't Care Less"

-date unknown-
{song}

you say now that you have changed and you want me back again
yet since the day you left me your heart I've tried to win
yes I've begged you and even cried a little I guess
but now my dear the tide has turned, I just couldn't care less
this whole time we've been apart I prayed I could forget you
well now I finally have, and no more will I be blue
you go your way, and I'll go mine, for all concerned it's best
for right now the way I feel, I just couldn't care less
maybe I should say I'm sorry, but that would be telling a lie
you are the one who walked out without even saying why
now my dear the future is yours, here's hoping you'll be blessed
but as far as you're concerned, I just couldn't care less

"A Lesson In Love"

5-16-61

if your heart has been
broken by the love of your life
by someone you cherish
and hoped would be your wife
listen to the voice of experience
one who knows sorrow and strife

if this my friend, has happened to you and you feel your life giving slack
slow your stride, repair your heart, you're a victim of love's fast track
this kind of love so rarely comes, passionate desires must be held back
the joyful reaping of the harvest, is to save the best for last
much like a business or a country, that's been witnessed in the past
love must have a good foundation, it won't stand if built too fast
to cure the ills and heal the wounds, requires nurturing, work, and time
living fast means loss of touch, dreams and goals are left behind
so slow your pace and let love work your rewards will be sublime

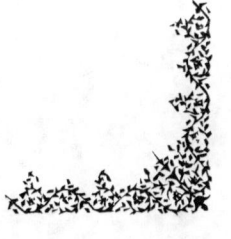

"The Easy Way Out"
2-11-63
{song}

I called you up last night to see if you could take a ride
and when he answered the phone I almost cried
I wanted to tell him that his wife was mine
but I hung up the phone and left him on the line

I could not help thinking, what he knew about,
or, what would happen when he found out
I knew better than to call the second time
and to come by would be way out of line

so I walked the lonely streets of town that night
and I was still walking when dawn broke first light
though all my thoughts my darling were of you
praying that what we had, was not through

then I saw a sign that read, take the easy way out,
go by air
so I purchased a one – way ticket to
heaven knows where
anywhere without you would make me blue
but to stay and wreck your world wasn't smart
and it was left for me to choose
so I took the easy way out of your heart
the easy way is always best for me
my heart gets too involved
and the blues won't let me be for I live on the back streets
and our love's so far apart
I knew I could never have you
so I took the easy way out of your heart

"Don't Fool With Danger"

4-7-70
{song}

don't fool with danger you know nothing of
a strange man is danger if he doesn't know love
he's looking for love to beg, borrow or steal
and if you are his victim your heart it will kill

so many women would be different today
if not for such a man somewhere along the way
they looked in his eyes then suddenly found
like the web of a spider so tight they're bound

they're bound to a love that could never be true
if you don't watch your step it will happen to you
no don't fool with danger you know nothing of
a strange man is danger if he doesn't know love

love to a stranger is something unreal
no heart has the stranger, no feelings to feel
don't be a fool; stop now while you can
I'm trying to tell you I am such a man

you don't get wet from not standing in the rain
hurting comes easy when you don't feel the pain
I'll give you fair warning, not one word more
then do as you wish, the choice is yours

"Benbush"

{on a Saturday night} 1-19-14
{song}

(begin with chorus)
I have been to Benbush on a Saturday night
Benbush girls know how to treat you right
serve up some "shine" an wrap your lovin' tight
you gotta go to Benbush on a Saturday night
– guitar run –
Benbush girls learn young and they know just how to please
if you're not on the same page they'll bring you to your knees
there ain't no doubt about it son you'll know if you've been squeezed
cause they got a law in Benbush no-one's allowed to tease

now they're just like good liquor only a whole lot quicker
and you really got it made if you are a guitar picker
they're always making candy and they'll use you for the mixer
now when it comes to candy she likes her's a whole lot thicker
they've got rockets in their pockets and ready for flight
they are built for speed and know how to use it right
and if you're not ready for-em you're going to die from fright
yeah man, you better hit Benbush on a Saturday night
(end with chorus)

"I Picked Up the Wrong End Again"

3-14-14
{song}

it's the story of my life – someone else's wife
yeah, I picked up the wrong end again

oh I picked up the wrong end again
knowing my heart was on the mend

I would never get sober
until it was all over
then I'd pick up the wrong end again

oh I picked up the wrong end again
when I'm drinking – I never play to win

I never think about pain
I just drive down lovers Lane
then I pick up the wrong end again

oh I picked up the wrong end again
knowing just how it's going to end

yes I love having fun
cause it keeps me on the run
so I'll pick up the wrong end again

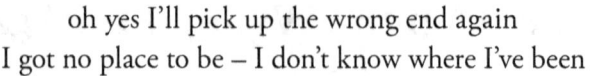

oh yes I'll pick up the wrong end again
I got no place to be – I don't know where I've been

until I die or get shot
I'm gonna give it all I've got
yes I'll pick up the wrong end again
oh yes I'll pick up the wrong end again!!!

"Raining From My Georgia Skies"

9-7-73
{song}

every time I think of Atlanta
I can see your big brown eyes
and when I see that Georgia rain coming down
I remember the many times I cried
oh – so many times – I cried

oh – you left me here in Atlanta
to that "ole" Windy City you did go-- and you know
there's nothing more lonesome than a Georgia night
when you are dreaming-of your darlin', in Chicago-o-o
chorus
so baby – come back home to Atlanta
don't let our love pass by
for when the wind disturbs the Chicago clouds
honey it's raining-- from my Geor--gia skies

well I never asked you for reasons
but the truth is—I- miss you so

if you don't bring your – love – back to Atlanta
I guess I'll have to find my way – to Chicago-o-o

if I go up north to Chicago-I might catch pneumonia-oh
I might catch pneumonia and die
and baby when I'm gone –will-- you come home
when they lay me- beneath these Georgia skies

oh baby- come on back home to Atlanta
please don't let our love pass by
for when the wind is blowing hard in Chicago
honey you know-- it's raining-- yes it's raining-- from my Ge-or--gia skies

"Sweet Young Country Girl"

7-26-71
{song}

she was a good "God" – fearing sweet young country girl
until I introduced her to my world
yes I'm to blame for her shame
and for her slandered name
"God" help this good "God" – fearing sweet young country girl
they are the devil's delight, and the snakes crawl at night
just searching for these good "God" – fearing sweet young country girls
her picture painted like a dream,
unlike she had ever seen
"God" help this good "God"-fearing sweet young country girl
I watched her take her place in my world

she played the part and lived the dream
she was perfect for my scheme
she thought I could do no wrong
she fell for every line that came along

now her shame is on my shoulders
and it makes me feel much older
"God" help this good "God"-fearing sweet young country girl
yes I'm to blame for her shame,
and for her slandered name
"God" help this good "God"-fearing sweet young country girl

"One Weakness"

1967

{song}

as strong as an ox, as big as a tree-e-e-e
as wise as "ole" Solomon, a leader like he
these things are in common, with the man you now see
but they say I have one weakness, and it's got the best of me
(chorus)
my weakness is women, they do strange things to me
though they're all the same, each one is different you see
to be true to one, I could never ever be
always on the run, it's the weakness in me

I've had girls from Alabama, Minnesota, Tennessee
Kentucky North Carolina, and Washington DC
my only trouble is, I love them all the same way
when my weakness set-in, it came to stay
– music run-
when I meet a new girl, she is the love of my life
and it seems to invite them, to start feeling like a wife
then I have to explain, that I was just born for fun
and if they are thinking of marriage, I'm not the -one-
cause my weakness is women, I love them one and all
I like making them happy, and answering when they call

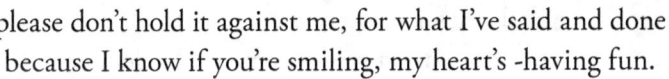

please don't hold it against me, for what I've said and done
because I know if you're smiling, my heart's -having fun.

yes my weakness is women, and blessed I may be
I'm always looking for fun, to feed the weakness in me
so if you walk into my life, you won't be there long
but while you are here, you'll sing happy song's
(end with chorus)

"Someone I Knew"

1-11-92

someone I knew, who feels good like you do
when you lay beside me, and I make love to you

you wait for my lead, like you haven't a clue
yes, you remind me, of someone I knew

someone I knew, who smells nice like you do
when love time is over, and night dreams come true

a glowing beauty, begins showing through
yes, you remind me, of someone I knew

when memories of sweetness, lose loving sounds
as we lie there together, I smile looking down

I can't help but wonder, at the wonders of you
yes, you remind me, of someone I knew

someone I knew, who filled my needs and desires
an eternal flame, was her love's burning fire

an all – around lover, and a real lady too
yes, you remind me, of someone I knew

someone I knew, who lived her life for me
my memories of her presence, are as real as can be

her compassion, her honesty, her feelings so true
yes, you remind me, of someone I knew

hese are memories we made, that I vowed to keep
each night they come calling, to me in my sleep

I promised forever, to her memory, I'd be true
yes, you remind me, of someone I knew
you remind me because, you're her memory too!!!

"Don't Take Her"

2-15-62

stay away from that girl, she's the girl of my dreams
she's all I've ever wanted and all I'll ever need

so please, stay away, don't take her with you
I know if she'd leave me my heart would break in two

it may sound silly, but why I don't know for I know
I would cry, if she were to go

please leave her alone, I'm begging you to
if you should leave with her, I wouldn't know what to do

the thought of loneliness, I know I could never bare
to know that her sweet caress, would no longer be there

so don't tempt her with promises, you know you can't keep
for she's the girl in my dreams, that makes me cry in my sleep

"Mr. Heartache"

12-5-63

yes I'll come to your party but be careful what you say
I've had a slight misfortune, and Mr. heartache passed my way
so with all consideration please don't mention her name
you see I'm trying to recover, by pretending it's a game
just a game I played and lost, they say these things happen every day
I never dreamed when it happened to me it would affect me this way
and when I get to your party be careful how you talk
don't say anything to remind me of the path I used to walk
those memories I do not need, it already hurts too much
and I fall apart every time I get the slightest memory of her touch
I just don't seem to be able to stand up and face the world
I guess it's because my heart was wrapped up in that girl
now that she's gone I must live on, this I tell myself each night
but there's just no way of telling, when an old memory might strike
so if I come to your party, please be careful what you say
then maybe I can make it through, to face another day

"Lay Your Lovn' Down"

7-1-78
{song}

I've been waiting for tonight ever since you left a
nd now it's finally here and I can't help myself
chorus
lay your lovin' down spread it all around
baby hear my plea
and put the hurt on me
you know you got to lay your lovin' down
the fever is raging from my head to my toe
a little voice inside sayin' go go go
lay your lovin' down you got the best in town
so spread it all around
you know you've got to lay your lovin' down
– piano run –
you know I've been a sufferin' since you went away
so before you go again you're gonna hear me say

lay your lovin' down make some lovin' sounds
before you vacate you know I can't wait
you'd better lay your lovin' down

it's the right time to tell you I'm glad you're back
and if you don't make a move I'm about to attack
now if you don't pursue I'm gonna come unglued
you know you always keep me in the mood
so lay your lovin' down you got the best around
aw- baby- hear my plea
and put the hurt on me
you know you've got to lay your lovin' down
– guitar run –
[end with chorus]

When Someone Beaks The Bad News To Me

4-13-66
{song}

there is a tall tall tale, going 'round town
that the things you've been doing, are a sin
they say lately, you have been seen dear
in the arms of so many different men

chorus
well if it's the truth, I wish you'd hide it
someplace where no---one can see
for you couldn't realize, how much it hurts dear
when someone breaks, the bad – news to me

I know I haven't been the best man,
but I've tried no – matter, what they say
and I can't help thinking, that you love me
no I don't believe the things I heard today

guitar run
you look just like an angel, when you hold me
and you tell me, our love's the perfect kind
then I heard, you were seen tra---ding bar-stools
trouble is, I heard it, from a r-e-a-l g-o-o-d friend of mine

chorus
oh – – if it's the truth, for my sake hi-d-e it
someplace where no – one can see
you just couldn't realize, how much it hurts dear
when someone breaks, the bad – news to me

no you couldn't realize, how much it hurts dear
when someone breaks, the bad – news to me!!!

"Without Saying Goodbye"

10-16-88
[song]

everything's still-- the same here, darlin' since you've—been-gone
and I am still ri--ght here waiting, honey for you-to come home
my neighbors all tell me, that I'm living a lie
but all I know is you left, without saying goodbye
your pictures – and knickknacks, still have their place – in our room
and there's a lock on – the door, to hol—d in – the gloom
I suppose when – I told you, that I would love you – until I died
I didn't plan on – you leavin', without saying goodbye
[chorus]
you left me holdin', something I couldn't stand
now my tears are rollin' down from the heart – land
no I don't care to listen, or to understand why
all I know is you left, without saying goodbye

you left me pictures of parties and so many – good times
things you thought I needed, to keep your memory alive
I have dreams of your body, all from head to toe
but I sure thought you'd tell me, goodbye if

you'd go
when I look at your legs, mercy, I see the twin towers
and climbing them – reminds me – I am under – your powers
oh the places – you took me, in two sec-onds flat when
it comes to lovin',e-m-m honey you are all that
{end with chorus}

"Don't Wake Me"

11-15-13
Song

don't wake me until the misery's gone
I don't need miseried moments hanging on

I've had good memories of her for so long
so don't wake me until the misery's gone

she was all I ever wanted, all I would ever need
the last thing on my mind was that she'd leave

not once did we argue, her love was a sweet song
so don't wake me until the misery's gone

I know that I will miss her, more than the air I breathe
just to be around her wakes up the life in me

I'm not ready to accept what she has done
so – don't wake me until the misery is gone

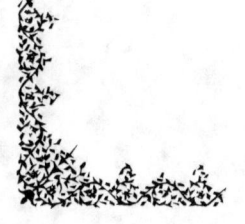

she was my love and happiness, personified
she filled my life with pleasure at my side

I'll just go to sleep and dream our love's still going on
no – don't wake me until the misery's gone

"Love And Farewell"

[toQueenie]
10-16-87
Song

don't make me hate you when I want to love you
like I have done all this time

don't turn me against the one that I need
and the one that I want to be mine

you make me wonder and you make me wish
for something sometimes my body cries

but lately I see a long distance look
of love and farewell in your eyes

by your absence I'm punished
for something I don't know I did

then you call me and tell me
you'll love me forever – again

while I think things are alright
and we're having a good night

in the morning you wake with a sigh
and a long distance look of love and farewell in your eyes

the taste of love dying, has kept us from trying
to bring back our feelings – a – new

you have different things now, to replace my love
and sometimes that makes me so blue

maybe I've been wrong, and my life is a sad song
all I know is I'm hurting like hell
I see you each time, not knowing if you're mine
with that long distance look of love and farewell

as I drive down the highway, I see things my
way but I don't know just what's on your mind

leaving or loving, pushing or shoving
but I know that I'm slipping behind

you tell me it's over, you don't really love me
then you wonder why I never cry

maybe this is the reason, my heart's out of season
it dies when I look in your eyes

and there lies the answer we both know so well
but we'll never tell

I'll live with your memory, and you'll have
that long distance look of love and farewell

with my heart full of love and my mind filled with memories
and you with that long distance look of love and farewell
"goodbye Queenie, I will miss you always"
lovingly, your *"Magic Man"*

"A Picture Of Me"

2-8-63

just look out your window, what do you see
you see a great – big picture of me

a whole lot of nothing, nobody nowhere
a whole lot of nothing, and no – one to care

now I cry my heart out, because of you
I cry all the time, since you said we're through

as I look from this window
my future seems dim

so I'll just keep on wondering
if you'll come back again

"She's Still Rockin' This Ship"
written twenty five years later on her birthday
3-28-12
[song]

well I went for a ride one Sunday morning
I didn't have--any place to go
I ended up--down by the ocean
why I was there--I guess she'll know

I built a big house, high on a hill
where I could talk – to the Whippoorwill
maybe it could tell me, where I should go
when it comes to findin' – my little darlin'
I found out--the Whippoorwill don't know
{chorus}
gonna rock this ship till I find my darlin'
I got nothing left but time
gonna rock this ship till I find my darlin'
cause she keeps burnin' up my mind

I went to see--a fortune – teller,
to find out--about my life
she said there's
someone--out there somewhere
that just can't wait – to be your wife
I was so happy--almost kissed her
just for mak--ing up that line
so I will search – the whole world over
for its her – that I must find

well I climbed up- on a haystack,
and dropped a needle – down inside
I started look-ing for that needle
but like you – the needle tries to hide

well I found it - late one evening,
and then – my search was through
you're harder than--a needle in a haystack,
honey I'm – still looking for you
{end with chorus}

"A Letter Of Teardrops"

2-11-63

I received a letter this afternoon, it makes the sixth one this week in
every letter I counted the teardrops that had fallen on each sheet

there must have been a hundred, or at least that many I know
I could tell by the starburst tear stained lines, they had not fallen slow

although the tears were faded and nearly dried away
each letter had a way of telling what her tears were trying to say

the first said, "my darling I love you, though you're so far away"
the second, "but I'll keep on praying that you will come back someday"
the third said, "I'm sorry we quarreled and then had to part"
then the fourth, "I realize now, it was my fault from the start"
the fifth said, "you know I still love you, and hope it can be"
finally, the sixth, "so please give mistakes to
the past, and tomorrow to me"

I sat there on my bed, with my head in my hands
I was trying o-o-h so hard, just to understand
for a while I was love – blinded, I couldn't think of what to say
because it really wasn't clear why I left that day

I had been gone for a month and thought I could forget
but now I realize, that I have not succeeded yet

during this time I met another, who was nothing short of a Queen
and it seems the time has come that I must choose between
o I answered her last letter, with a few lines across the top
and in it I returned some of my own teardrops

I said, "my dearest darling, I will always
love you, and you know it is true
but I'm so sorry, it's impossible, for one to be true to two
you will always have my heart, and darling, I want you to know
you will take my heart with you, wherever you may go"

although it was a contradiction, to lose her crushed my very soul
to spend my life with her had been my every goal
yet someone else in thirty days, the story could be told
that I was born to love, but never meant to hold

it might have been a favor, that I blessed her with, so bold
but now my future looks, so dark – so bleak – so cold
so I'll take what comes my way, or what life offers me
for those few years I had with her, were the best that there could be

"Brown Eyes Long Hair"

[bottles and pretty ladies] 4-19-70
{song}

Brown eyes, long – hair, bottles, and pretty ladies
lawd, have been the ruination of me
no, it isn't their fault, my ego is slipping
and it's moral support that I need
when I was just a young man not hardly full-grown
I lacked confidence and faith of my own
so with my pride arrested my talents I tested
and I entered another man's home
I chose the back streets of life and other men's wives
and with lust for the wild-life I'd cry
a lot of hearts were torn
bad habits were formed
but I couldn't stop it if I'd try
chorus
Brown eyes, long – hair, bottles and pretty ladies
Lawd, have been the ruination of me
no, it isn't their fault, my ego is slipping
and it's moral support that I need

when you've lived life the way I do, there is no true love for you
you can't trust people, even when you want too
the very best that you can hope for
is to love a little more
and try not, to get caught, doin' what you do

"Think About Me"

(when you're lonely)
7-6-2008

that rain just keeps on fallin'
floods my miseried- mildewed mind

floats a memory of a loved – one
who has left me far behind

please think about me when you are lonely
would you speak my name from time to time

I want never to forget you
though you leave lonesome, on my mind

I recall so clearly, the day you left me
with the look of love still on your face

I have wished one-thousand times and over
that you would return to take your place

so promises that you won't forget me
allow my dreams one final try

to capture my eternal heart – throb
and give you love that will not die

The Tears On My Pillow Never Dry

9-18-07
[song]

oh the tears on my pillow never dry
{they won't dry}
and you are the reason, baby, you're the reason why
ever since you left, it's been so easy to cry
that the tears on my pillow never dry
{no they won't dry}

you're like a sad movie that plays on and on
and keeps dropping heartaches like a never ending song
filled with pain and sorrow, "God" only knows why
and the tears on my pillow never dry, {they won't dry}
you left me standin' here, with nothin' to hold but a beer
when the tears on my pillow won't dry
people, look at me and wonder why
all they ever see me do is sigh
they don't seem to understand
just what happens to a man
when the--tears on his pillow won't dry
{baby they won't dry}
no the tears on my pillow never dry—{they won't dry}
and you are the reason, baby, you're the reason why
ever since you left, it's been so easy to cry
oh you left me standin' here, with nothin' to hold but a beer
and the tears on my pillow just won't dry
no the tears on my pillow never dry

"I Love To Dream"
11-23-71

now I never picked peaches in Georgia
and I didn't lumber – Jack in Maine
but I did get caught by a pretty little girl
and I had to change her name
but I wiggled free
aw, lucky me
back in West Virginia everything was peaches and cream
on a far away highway I hear a truck coming my way
and I had to realize a dream
I'm leaving fast
to get away from my past
hangin' round Detroit city, just chillin' in an old box-car
I ran into Bobby Bare
who claimed residence there
so I shared that train with the star
but I'm leaving fast
while the spirits last
I headed out to L.A. with sunshine on my mind
I got side – tracked in Vegas
things there were so outrageous
I lost the rest of my behind
now I'm leaving fast
running out of cash
I've been beach bummin' with bikinis
clinging to the back of my head
damn, if I keep dreamin' like this
I might actually get a kiss
have a heart attack or wind up dead
I'm not leaving, this place is a blast
and I'm out of gas

beaches, bikinis, and love-ins, that appeals to me
I think I'll stay here a while
learn to surf and change my style
or maybe just drift on out to sea
hey, this place is cool
I hain't no fool
and "God," I l-o-v-e to dream

"Down Memory Row"

1-19-14
{song}

I'm singing my way down memory row
I've been lots-a-places, and many more to go
if I'm running behind, it's because I'm slow takin'
my time, singing my way--down memory row

well I don't want to miss you
I remember when I kissed you
singled out in the courthouse
you were quiet as a mouse

except the way you dressed
made me want to caress
what you were trying to hide
sort-a-tore me up inside

those jeans and that sweater
could not have fit any better
you couldn't hide in the crowd
your jeans were walkin' proud

I don't know where you got –em
but anyone could tell
from the top to the bottom
you wore them oh so well

I'm sure it came as no surprise
that you had really caught my eye
you had that perfect way of Struttin'
and your legs went up--to your belly button

your beauty seemed to shine
it very nearly put me blind
the look on your face came right on time
you knew I was lov-ing you--in my mind

I can see you liked it nice and slow
and we both knew where this would go
but I'm telling you things you already know
takin' my time, singing my way--down memory row

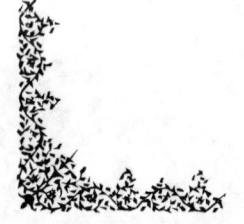

"Brand-new Birthday Blues"

{fifty years later}
1-27-1

your love has been a real good teacher
it left me sitting in times bleachers

watching other people having a good time
and thinking about when you were mine

but don't worry darling, you did all you could do
I really didn't know, what I had in you

oh it's my fault baby, I'll take the blame
and I will spend the rest of my life in shame

without you I can never be happy again
knowing I caused our love to end

oh, but I'll get along baby, and I'll be fine
in this "ole" one-way-world of mine

where all my memories, taste like candy and
heartaches, well, they're always handy

oh, in every corner your face I see
reminding me, that I couldn't see

the forest for the trees
until they all fell on me

and the grass is greener over yonder
but once I got there I began to wonder

why did I leave what I once had
that must be why I feel so bad

woman get your clutches out of me
cut those chains and set me free

"lawd", don't leave me here so sad
with a memory of what I once had

then I'll be all right, yes I'll be fine
in this "ole" one- way- world of mine

tomorrow comes and the blues will go
must have been the moon that hurt me so

more likely, too much Jack Daniels got in my way
since I'm writing this for you on your birthday

oh, but don't worry about me, cause I'll be fine
it's just another chapter, in this one- way -world of mine
"HAPPY BIRTHDAY BABY"

"Love Questions #2"
9-16-13

until my life is one with history
it shall be for me a mystery

for the love I took shall I receive
the frigid cold of winters eve

until the fire inside me dies
and claims victory for my demise

or hold your love for sweet surprise
with wish for warmth within me rise

questions always in one's mind
belief and trust is hard to find

did she love me as I loved her
unimportant now 'tis all a blur

when my life takes its final course
will I have pain with no remorse

has left me now a heart-so-sore
I look at death and say no-more

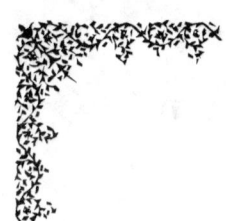

"Thanks-Love"

5-29-80

love you've been good to me
lead me to, and through, lots of misery

kept me up so many sleepless nights
love, I wish I could've treated you right

it could be my heart, or my head
maybe I didn't mean a word I said

I'd throw you away time after time
you'd start me over and not seem to mind

all the loves you gave me were good
I screwed them up like you knew I would

before it got to the point where things were done
you were waiting right there with another one

you were always forgiving of my mistakes
with a constant supply of hearts to break

life's been so much fun I'd like to do it over
for I know you'd keep me rolling in clover

love, if I wore a hat I would tip it to you
you have been a friend my whole life through

and now in my autumn, I say seriously
<u>thank you Love, for taking care of me</u>

Looks A Whole Lot Better Leavin'

7-20-11
{song}

well I'm all coffee'd up, and baby I'm headed out a town
I got business elsewhere, and I am Virginia bound
but I want to tell you this, and honey, you best be believin'
this "ole" town looks a whole lot better when you're leavin'
aw—this "ole" town looks a whole lot better when you're leavin'
when I pass that city limit sign I won't be grievin'
well I may make it back someday
– but I don't plan to stay
cause this "ole" town looks a whole lot better when you're leavin'
I've been here two weeks, and "Lord" it feels like a year
this place drove me back to drinkin', and I'm gonna have another beer
when I give you back your town
I'll be frowning up – side – down
cause this "ole" town looks a whole lot better when you're leavin'
it has some nice people, but they don't think I am a human – being
they think I'm a little strange,
and I think they're deranged
yeah, this "ole" town looks a whole lot better when you leavin'
well there's two thousand people, and three funeral home
in case you're wondering, what I'm trying to get away from
well it's not what you're leavin', but what you're going to
and leavin' this place, is what I gotta do
it's that "ole" rebel's heart, that's making me walk the line
and when I cross into Virginia, my heart's on double time
just to know I finally got what I've been needin'
oh – this "ole" town looks a whole lot better when you're leavin'
when I passed that city limit sign, I was not grievin'

I'm giving you back your town,
while I'm frowning upside down
yeah, this "ole" town looks 100% better when you're leavin'
{baa—do-be-do-wa}
yeah, this "ole" town looks a whole lot better when you're leavin'

"Put A Bell On My Bottle"

1965-66
{song}

chorus
just put a bell on my bottle
and let me ring you when I'm dry
I'm in a booth back in the corner
all alone so I can cry
my darling's gone – I lost my heart
and now I'm gonna lose my mind
so put a bell on my bottle
and let me ring you when I'm dry

yeah – put a bell on my bottle
and let me ring you when I'm dry

I don't want to be bothered
all I want to do is cry

I should have known better
than treatin' her this way

now she's gone – – it's lonesome at home
and this is the price I pay
end with chorus

"The All American Drunk"

1958
Song

gather round "cats" and you shall hear
how to digest the smell of beer
buy you a bottle round about noon
you will be swaying and staggering soon
mixin' hot lips with all that wine – yeah

well I bought me a bottle about a week ago
I learned how to drink in an hour or so
and all around town it was understood
that I was just a drunk and no damn good
gettin' drunk, all the time – yeah

well I drank all day and way up in the night
and my pappy's hair was turnin' white
you see, he didn't like me starting to drink
he said, "you can stay son, but that stuff stinks,
it's gotta go boy" yeah

so I picked up my bottle, stopper and all
and I bid farewell to my poor old "pa"
I split for Memphis where they say "you – all"
those swingin' drunks were having a ball
drinking sessions, wine bottles and all-yeah

I was rocking them bottles, they were about to break
the women all said that I had the shakes
then up stepped the sheriff with a great big grin
he said," listen here soak, I'm gonna run you in
I'll put you in the jailhouse boy, give you a big long bed"-yeah

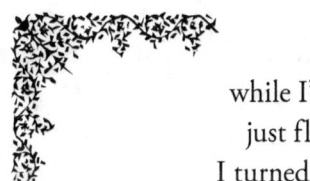

while I'm sleepin' all night in that "ole" bed
just flippin' the cockroaches off my head
I turned my hide – away bottle up with a grin
and the wine just kept on pourin' in
and then one day my Uncle Sam
he starts to rattle my cage sayin' "here I am
your Uncle Sam needs you boy"
I said "Uncle Sam I'm sorry to tell
I'm the prize possession of this county jail"-- yeah

"Illegal Brew"

7-3-11
{song}

checkin' my mirrors, watching those side roads
screamin' down the mountain, with a brew overload

those mountain "Mounties", got nothing to do
except stop you from runnin', a little illegal brew

there's a stretch from Strasburg, to the "ole" corridor-
H and that's just about the only, place your safe

when you leave Virginia, and hit the mountain state
you can't make up time, if you're running late

cause if you get caught speedin', then the search is on
and if they find what you got, you'll be a long time gone

and those state boys', they're everywhere
they come out-a your trunk, and drop from the air

ya gotta try to get through'em, if you can
you can sell your brew, if you beat the man

take your share from the middle, you can straighten out the road
if you get there before them, you get paid for your load

makin' that "ole" beer run, you carry illegal brew
from Virginia through the mountains, they're gonna catch you
well it's a dangerous game, with these aluminum cans
playin' hide and seek, ya-know you gotta have a plan

when you know someday, you'll play a losing hand
and you'll be doin' time, if you're caught by the man

runnin' that "ole" beer, a lotta illegal brew
with a little excitement, just to carry ya-through

Think Maybe I'll Find Myself Here

1968
{song}

I've been searching all the back streets, bar rooms and lonely cafés
trying to find where I left me, oh – where did I lose my way

in every glass of beer I hold in my hands, I search every bubble for cheer
trying to find me and take back command,
think maybe I'll find myself here

oh – what would it take for this glass to break and spill all over the floor
I'd be so easy to find with nothing to hide behind,
yeah – think maybe I'll find myself here

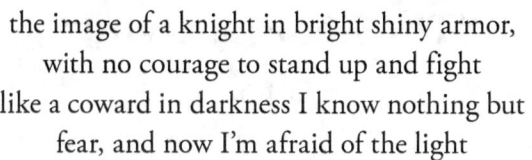

the image of a knight in bright shiny armor,
with no courage to stand up and fight
like a coward in darkness I know nothing but
fear, and now I'm afraid of the light

oh – what would it take for this class to break and spill all over the floor
I'd be so easy to find with nothing to hide behind,
think maybe I'll find myself here
when a woman leaves you all alone the bar and bottle is your home
and you are lost like driftwood on the sea
you try to find some comfort here
in this "ole" bar just drinking beer
oh – think maybe I can find myself here oh what would
it take for this glass to break, and spill all over
the floor
I'd be so easy to find, with nothing to hide behind
think maybe I'll find myself here,
oh – do you think – – we can find ourselves here
y-e-a-h think maybe I'll find myself here

"The Fear Of Dying"
4-1-62

this fear of dying that we know is inherent of Earth's first man
with no weapons for daily protection he engaged his foes by hand
medicine was unheard of at the time and doctors there were none
even being the conqueror, the struggle to live was the hardest one
it seems strange, nothing's changed, staying
alive is still our main concern
generation after generation we work and kill, the lust for life we yearn
by inventions and discoveries our lives have been extended
the longer we live the more we strive to live longer than intended
if we live one thousand years this fear of dying would remain
our number one priority though ultimately, <u>in vain!!!</u>

"Gonna Drink Up All The Beer"
10-16-87.
{song}

Tonight I'm gonna drink up all the beer
they can make up in Milwaukee for the next 500 years
my baby left me sad and my heart hurts so bad
so tonight I'm gonna drink up all the beer

she took the Corvette and the cats, and my bank accounts are flat
so tonight I'm gonna drink up all the beer
yes tonight I'm gonna drink up all the beer
they can make up in Milwaukee for the next 500 years
I'll find a booth by that back wall, and I'll drink till I can't crawl
cause tonight I'm gonna drink up all the beer

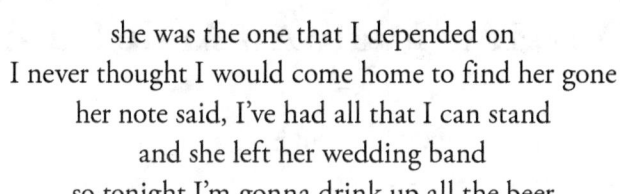

she was the one that I depended on
I never thought I would come home to find her gone
her note said, I've had all that I can stand
and she left her wedding band
so tonight I'm gonna drink up all the beer

yes tonight I'm gonna drink up all the beer
they can make up in Milwaukee for the next 500 years
I'll buy a roll of paper towels and fill them up with
tears cause tonight I'm gonna drink up all the beer
she said," no one could have ever loved you more
but this is now, and that's the way it was before
I'm leavin' you like you left me, all alone in misery
and a Dear-John note hanging on your door"

so tonight I'm gonna drink up all the beer
they can make up in Milwaukee for the next 500 years
crying time is about to start, and I'm gonna play my part
for tonight I'm gonna drink up all the beer
[if song-repeat last verse here} after – help me out now
{choruses are enter-mingling}

West Virginia Made An Alkie Out-A-Me

7-2-12
{song}

West Virginia you are so wild and free
And you are just as boring as you can be
your moonshine has ruined my knees
WV you made an alkie out-a-me

I loved your women, they like to dream
I don't like your mountains, or your streams
well that's my problem, from what I can see
WV you made an alkie out-a-me

the only thing good in these hills
comes in a jar, and it will kill
well it's moonshine, grapevine, white lightning
too you might as well drink, there's nothing else to do

it takes too much time, to drive around your mountains
and everywhere you look, there's a moonshine fountain
but worst of all, are things you can't resist
like a mountain mama, beggin' to be kissed

you know I always liked a little surf and turf
but venison and trout hain't heaven on earth
now cow crap and a barn, is the country way
but I'll take concrete and high-rises, any day

so you can keep your mountains, and your streams
and I'll go back to the city, where the nightlife gleams
-music run-
I came here for a visit, after many many years
and when I tried to leave, I realized my fears

they don't make white lightning, in Washington
and the only kind of shine, comes from the sun
you can't get that grapevine, down in "ole" DC
yeah West Virginia, you made an alkie out-a-me

Alcohol – From My Head To My Toe

2-6-66
{song}

chorus
alcohol from my head to my toe, if they took a
blood test that's all that would show.
Now I'm just as numb as a hundred and one, but
I'll tell you boys I have a whole bunch of fun.

Now this old heart's had a whole lot of aches, and
this old heart has had its share of breaks.
Well there ain't nothing it can't take cause it's stimulated by alcohol.
chorus

when my sweet mama gets mad at me, she beats
me black and blue till I can hardly see.
But it don't hurt none when I have to crawl,
cause I'm plum numb from alcohol.

Now I went out drinkin' just last night, and I met
a little gal that was wrapped real tight.

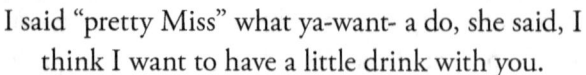

I said "pretty Miss" what ya-want- a do, she said, I
think I want to have a little drink with you.

I said I guess I reckon one drink won't hurt, so
I spilled my drink all over her skirt.
she took it off and I loaned her my shirt, but I didn't get cold at all.
Cause I test a 100 proof alcohol.
chorus
e partied all night until the bars closed down,
just slippin' an sliddin' all over that town.
Hidin' from the cops when they came around,
trying to find a place to lay our bodies down.

When I finally got her home she was such a mess,
I tried to tell her husband that I done my best.
He shook my hand and then he shot me down,
now I'm spilling alcohol all over the ground.
Chorus

now I'm nearly dead at 26, but up until now
I've been gettin' my kicks [-on-]
[chorus--slower&lower]

The Bottles Are Empty – The Tables Are Bare

5 –16 –71
{song}

the bottles are empty and the tables are bare
and there's not a soul around here that cares

I've got no one to listen to me while I cry
and there is a heartache inside that just won't pass by
chorus
somebody, somebody listen to me
I'm not a loner I need company
now the bartender told me I can't buy no more time
I am taking too long to drink her off my mind

yeah the bottles are empty and the tables are bare
and there's big pool of pity around here somewhere

oh if I could just find it I would jump in and drown
then I won't be crying when her memory comes around

{guitar run}
well I don't fear dying but I can't be alone
and the house that I go to is no longer a home

so help me bartender let me have just one more
I need lots a of courage to make it to the door

yeah the bottles are empty and so is my life
but it's not my fault it's because of my wife

she left me this morning and won't take my call
now the tears on my table are pure alcohol
{end with chorus}

"No Room In My Belly For A Beer"

2008
{song}

there's no room in my belly for a beer
we went out to eat, and got filled up to our ears
I'm so broken – hearted an sad
for a beer I have not had
now there's no room in my belly for a beer
we stopped by Costco's sample stands
taking samples with both hands
now there is no room in my belly for a beer
our next stop was the Golden Corral
I think I ate a whole dang cow
and there's no room in my belly for a beer
when we got all filled up
we filled our pockets for the pups
and Joe said let's get out of here
or I will face my greatest fear
there'll be no room in my belly for a beer
{next day}, now there's room in my belly for a beer
I'm in the shower, would you bring it to me dear
I just can't wait to pop that top
and guzzle down that slop – hops,-sloppy- hops
now there's room in my belly for a beer!
I don't even know what hops is
but I love beer, beer for president – – yeah!!!

Rooster

1966
{song}

When I was just a young boy, not even in my teens,
mama took the bottle away, and said now you been weaned;
she said you're getting older, and there's lots of things that's new,
so I started in by drinking up, a gallon of Paw's homebrew;
as time went by, the changes came, slowly as they should,
so I started drinking Lighting, and it tasted mighty good;
I've drank so dad – burned many kinds, I can't remember names,
so I just call –em rooster, for to me they're all the same; chorus
I love my rooster, my rooster loves me; it makes me happy,
so happy and free; we're sticking together, whatever may be;
and we'll always be happy, my rooster and me;

now I'm a little older and I took a darlin' wife,
she vowed that she would love me for the rest of her dear life;
it seems a little funny and I can't believe it's true,
but to me and my "ole rooster", that sweet gal said I do;
we've got such darlin' children, to me they are a treat,
I bring them up on rooster juice, cause we very seldom eat;
some kids would not appreciate a father of this sort,
but they all love me and understand, they call me "rooster" for short;
chorus
if you should ever meet me or pass me on the street,
you must not be surprised if I fall at your feet;
just stick around and watch cause I'll get up again,
for me and my "ole rooster", in the end we always win;
when it comes time for me to die, all I ask is please,

just place a gallon of rooster right in along-side of me;
we ain't used to being parted and I wouldn't look my best,
if I didn't have my rooster when they laid me down to rest:
{end with chorus}

"The Wanton Of Death"

1961

come ye, Oh welcomed spirits,
enter with a will thine own;
into this old shackled body,
that wrappest' round my bones;
for 'tis all that still remains,
of what was once a man;
I try to walk then find out I,
'tis difficult to but stand;
I invite you oh spirits,
from the heavens I pray thou dost come;
but if the devil must have my soul,
then even hell I shall accept as home;
it matters not the consequence,
'tis this body, it suffers great;
so comest thou quick oh comforting spirits,
for 'tis with more than much agony I await;
surround me thou lifeless friends,
as the beasts surround their prey;
I shall pretend I see thee not,
while upon my bed I lay;
I confess to thee, my friendly foes,
whom I have fought and feared for years;
need I say too, the thought of you,
brought many hours of fear;
but my body groweth weaker,

as the years didst come and go;
I find too, in this old shackled lump,
fear of you has ceased to grow;
must I say more thou successor of life,
while I envision the whitest cloud;
clear up thou mind, So densely fogged,
and speakest thee aloud;
this vision you did show,
its form 'twas like a dove;
ah yes, it cometh clear,
my ghost it is, hovering above
clutch me oh long awaited one,
for 'tis you I long to meet;
through this life I've lived, this is the first,
to need invite defeat;
I have peaked the highest mountains,
I have topped the tallest trees;
'twas this way then but now I must submit,
to you death, whom at last have conquered me;
O death, you dreadful death,
what keepest thee away;
why dost thou linger oh heartless one,
when so helplessly I lay;
you are indeed of much contempt,
my curses thou hast won;
yet even still of thee I beg,
let this lifeless life be done;
let this be, oh taker of life,
a lovely last and never ending night;
come, enter herein oh death,
and send my sin-filled soul aflight;
I have no time to argue,
no strength left in me;
'tis not defeat that I face now,
but an endless victory;
oh death, is this you now that I dost feel,

as your clutches around me break;
your hands so gentle as from me,
this worthless life they take;
many thanks to thee, O death,
whom I thought had forgotten me;
but now I find my soul ascending,
into an everlasting, eternity!!!

Sorry to leave you with such morbid thoughts.
But death should always be last… <u>I Think</u>
But after all that beer, you never know!

Maybe the next volume will have a more appealing ending.
But then again, maybe not, I guess we'll have to wait and see

www.ingramcontent.com/pod-product-compliance
Lightning Source LLC
Chambersburg PA
CBHW052034070526
44584CB00016B/2036